CH00763595

Shifting Sands and Solid Rock

Religious Life in a Changing World

Patricia Jordan, FSM

GRACEWING

First published in 2015

Gracewing
2 Southern Avenue
Leominster
Herefordshire HR6 0QF

ISBN 978 0 85244 869 4

Typeset by Action Publishing Technology Ltd
Gloucester GL1 5SR

Shifting Sands
and Solid Rock

Contents

Contents

Dedication

With loving gratitude to
Sr Kathleen Moffatt, OSF
Friend and Mentor to our Congregation

And

To all those
I have had the privilege to accompany
on their Vocation Journey

Acknowledgements

At the beginning of the Year of Consecrated Life, I express my heartfelt gratitude to the sisters in my Congregation for the way in which they have encouraged and nurtured my growth in understanding my Franciscan vocation. In particular, I thank the sisters in my local community for their enthusiasm and willingness to continue the search to enter more deeply into the Mystery of our Gospel call, as we seek together to 'live differently', in the spirit of St Francis and St Clare. I am also deeply indebted to many men and women Religious (you know who you are) for friendship, inspiration and encouragement over many years.

My special thanks to Sr Elizabeth Ruth Obbard, ODC, for her unique illustrations which capture the theme of each chapter.

I express my gratitude to Tom Longford and Sr Mary Joseph, OSB, from Gracewing Publishing, for the help and support I have received in the process of having this book reach publication.

I acknowledge that all Biblical references are from *The New Jerusalem Bible Study Edition*, London: Darton, Longman & Todd, 1994.

Foreword

Remain, with resolute hearts, faithful to the Lord
(cf. Acts 11:23–24) and continue on this
journey of grace.

These words taken from *Keep Watch! A Letter to Consecrated Men and Women*,[1] for the Year of Consecrated Life, are words of encouragement and challenge as we try to live our lives steadfastly faithful in a fast changing world. As a follower of St Francis of Assisi, I am well aware that Francis showed the world an alternative way. In the midst of religious, political and social unrest and upheaval, Francis simply lived the Gospel. The Franciscan author, Richard Rohr, claims that there is a universal accessibility, invitation, and inclusivity in an authentic Franciscan spirituality. This is because Francis made the Gospel his rule of life. Once again, Pope Francis is reminding us that the Gospel is the 'ultimate norm and the supreme rule of Religious Life of all Institutes'.[2] Recognition of the variety of charisms is attributed to this evangelical inspiration. It is the Gospel that takes us back to the source of every life rooted in Christ.

On the Eve of the Year of Consecrated Life, Pope Francis addressed Religious in the Basilica of Saint Mary Major, reminding us always to use the Gospel as our starting point, translated into 'daily gestures marked by simplicity and coherence, avoiding the temptation to transform it into an ideology'. He also said that the Gospel keeps our life and mission 'young', thus keeping them 'current and attractive.' Ours is the call to be 'living exegeses of the Gospel', which is the foundation and final reference point of our life and mission.[3]

In *Keep Watch*, Pope Francis challenges us to live differently and to be like watchmen, working constantly at the junction between the Church and the world. He says that consecrated people have a unique role in reading and interpreting the signs of the times and go out to the peripheries of today's men and women. How each Institute will answer this call will depend on their God-given charism. 'Religious families are born to inspire new journeys, suggest unforeseen routes, or respond nimbly to human needs and necessities of the spirit'.[4] This is what our Founders and Foundresses did. This is our call now in the twenty-first century. To continue the journey we need 'the prophecy of watchfulness'.[5]

The aims of this year of grace are threefold: to gratefully remember our past, to live in the present with passion and to embrace the future with hope. Developing these themes at some length, Pope Francis invites us to be grateful that 'all our Institutes are heir to a history rich in charisms ... Remembering our past is essential for preserving our identity, for strengthening our unity as a family and our common sense of belonging.[6]

Called to live the present with passion is the most challenging of the aims of this Year. It is the challenge to love passionately. First, to fan into flame our personal

love for Jesus. Pope Francis asks: 'Is Jesus really our first
and only love, as we promised he would be when we
professed our vows?'[7] This in turn challenges us to a
concrete expression of this passionate love in our service
to others. We see here the emphasis on the 'mysticism of
encounter', which is deep and far-reaching, personal
and out-going.

The 'mysticism of encounter' will lead us 'to set out
anew, with trust in the Lord. Prophets receive from God
the ability to scrutinize the times in which we live and to
interpret events'.[8] With an emphasis on fraternity and
communion, Pope Francis challenges us to 'Go into all
the world', saying, 'A whole world awaits us: men and
women who have lost all hope, families in difficulty,
abandoned children, young people without a future, the
elderly, sick and abandoned, those who are rich in the
world's goods but impoverished within, men and
women looking for a purpose in life, thirsting for the
divine'.[9] This in turn challenges us to find new and
creative ways to proclaim the Gospel.

In *Keep Watch*, Pope Francis, in presenting us with the
story of the prophet Elijah and the symbolism of the
Exodus, highlights the mystical and prophetic dimensions of consecrated life. On a previous occasion, when
addressing the Major Superiors, he said that 'a Religious
must never abandon prophecy'. Now in this new
document, Pope Francis says, 'We are being presented
with the possibility of continuing our journey with
courage and watchfulness, so as to make daring choices
that will honour the *prophetic* character of our identity'.[10]
If we are to respond to the graces of this privileged
opportunity, we need to start anew in silent adoration,

with loving, listening hearts, fanning into flame our first love when Jesus warmed our hearts. Then and only then, will we be able to awaken in the hearts of others 'a thirst for the infinite'.[11] With passionate love, gratitude, and deep humility of heart, it is a privilege to acknowledge that 'a whole world awaits us'.

Hail Mary, Woman of the New Covenant,
grant us a prophet's voice to tell the world about the joy
of the Gospel, about the blessedness of those who search
the horizons of new lands and heavens (cf. Rev 21:1) and
anticipate their presence in the human city.[12]

Notes

1 Pope Francis, *Keep Watch! A Letter to Consecrated Men and Women Journeying in the Footsteps of God.* Congregation for Institutes of Consecrated Life and Societies of Apostolic Life. London: CTS, 2014.
2 Pope Francis, *Keep Watch!*, 8.
3 http://www.NCRegister.com/dailynews/AnnSchneible/ CAN/EWTNnews Date of Access 29.11.2014.
4 Ibid., 13.
5 Ibid., 10.
6 Pope Francis, *Message for the Year of Consecrated Life*, 29 November 2014, 1/1.
7 Ibid., 1/2.
8 Ibid., 1/3.
9 Ibid., 11/4.
10 Pope Francis, *Keep Watch!*, 1.
11 Ibid., 13.
12 Ibid., 19.

Introduction

This book is the result of a chance remark. How often the Lord speaks to us in the ordinary conversations we have with those who touch our lives on a daily basis. I was showing some visiting sisters from another Congregation around our House of Prayer and in the course of our conversation the topic of vocations came up. This led us into the deeper realms of conversation about lifestyle and charism. After an animated conversation, one of the sisters said: 'You should write a book'. The thought lingered in my mind and the desire grew in my heart to share something of the gift of Religious Life. I share from an angle that is very simple, though perhaps at times hidden in the midst of the many theories about Religious Life, its past and future, that have been explored especially since Vatican II.

I have lived through many changes in Religious Life during past decades. I have had to teach about Religious Life for the past thirty years because I have been in the ministry of Formation during the whole of that time. I have been engaged in every area of Formation Ministry: Vocation Discernment, Candidate Mistress, Postulant Mistress, Novice Mistress, Juniorate Mistress and Director of On-Going Formation for my Congregation. I have had to engage with many and varied theories, and assess them in the light of the sound teaching of the Church and the tradition of the centuries, as it has been lived and passed on from generation to generation. I have had to sift through the chaff and the wheat, and I have had to struggle with the on-going challenges that face every Religious Congregation to a greater or lesser degree. Through it all, I have a passion for Religious Life, the gift that it is to the one who receives it, and the gift it is to the Church and the world.

This book is born out of my own experience. Its limitations are mine and mine alone, but I hope and pray that those who are Religious, those who may be thinking about answering God's call, and those who may wish to know more about Religious Life in the Church, may find in it a kernel of truth to sustain them in their search and in their commitment to Jesus in a love that never ends.

In Chapter One, I explore with you the challenge of Vatican II through revisiting the Document on Religious Life: *Perfectae Caritatis*. This seems timely during this Year of Faith when Pope Benedict invites us to rediscover the riches of the Council's Documents. In addition I will refer to those two wonderful Documents given by Pope John Paul II on Religious Life: *Vita Consecrata* and *Starting Afresh from Christ*. My purpose is not to revisit what has been said many times already but to approach the challenge in the context of faith leading to perfect love.

Chapter Two will concentrate on the gift that is offered to some men and women to embrace a radical form of Christian living. We will unpack some of the scriptural references in *Vita Consecrata* which help to elucidate the call to Religious Life. These will be developed in the context of Franciscan Religious Life, with special reference to St Clare's self-understanding of her call to mystical espousal, spiritual motherhood and sisterhood.

Chapter Three will progress to identifying the different models of Religious Life: monastic, apostolic, evangelical. We will explore the implications for leadership, prayer, ministry and community, the consequences of which will naturally lead to a deeper understanding of religious identity. This will take us into the elusive and soul-searching area of Congregational charisms. Each Religious family will be encouraged to delve more deeply into the legacy of their Founder or Foundress and accept the challenge to embody the charism in a way that is always new in every person and in every era.

Chapter Four will look at the emergence of new groups of Religious since Vatican II, and also at ways in which older Congregations have renewed, or are renewing their lives in accordance with the invitations and challenges presented to them. This will lead to sifting and sorting the essentials from the non-essentials.

Finally, in Chapter Five, we are challenged by Pope Francis to 'wake up the world'. We arrive at a new place of breathtaking horizons which fan into flame the love that builds and grows on the Rock that is Christ. The shifting sands may come and go, but they shape and challenge us in their coming and going, having the potential to root us ever more deeply in Jesus Christ who is the same yesterday, today and forever. He is the Rock on which every vocation is founded and grounded. Keeping our eyes on Jesus is the focus underpinning this reflection on Religious Life. As you read and reflect, may you discover or rediscover what it means to fall in love with Jesus Christ, radically, totally and forever.

LOVE

INVITES

Chapter 1

A Crescendo of Love

I invite you in the first place to nourish a faith that can illuminate your vocation. For this I urge you to treasure, as on an inner pilgrimage, the memory of the 'first love' with which the Lord Jesus Christ warmed your hearts, not out of nostalgia but in order to feed that flame.

(Pope Benedict XVI)

The seed for this book was sown in the Year of Faith, inaugurated by Pope Benedict from October 2012 until November 2013. For me this is significant. In *Porta Fidei* Pope Benedict states:

Only through believing, then, does faith grow and become stronger; there is no other possibility for possessing certitude with regard to one's life apart from self-abandonment, in a continuous crescendo, into the hands of a love that seems to grow constantly because it has its origin in God.[1]

These words struck me as being very relevant to the way I see Religious Life today at the beginning of the twenty-first century. Since Vatican II perhaps some Religious, at a personal and Community level, have experienced a lack of certitude and a fear of abandoning oneself and one's Community into the hands of a loving God. There are many and varied reasons for this lack of certitude and the presence of fear. Numerous authors have written eloquently and convincingly about the future of Religious Life, oftentimes pointing to its demise or absolute discontinuity with what has gone before. Some have spoken of 'paradigm shifts' and in explaining how this phenomenon has affected Religious Life, they have adopted the language of anthropology, sociology, psychology, culture and philosophical theology, to name but a few. Whatever the perspective, all would agree that great changes have taken place. Predictions about the future have both enthused and challenged but also daunted and dismayed many Religious. While recognising this backdrop in attempting to write about Religious Life, I wish in this Year of Faith simply to explore Religious Life from the perspective of faith leading to perfect love. Perhaps this approach may prevent what Joan Chittester refers to as 'disillusionment by endless historical review of past forms of Religious Life and long excursions into futuristic speculation, as well'.[2] This has already been done in past decades.

Year of Faith

This Year of Faith (2012–2013) coincides with the fiftieth anniversary of Vatican II, and for me hints at a sense of Jubilee as we explore and celebrate the gift of Religious Life in the Church. Jubilee always begins with Sabbath rest, an inner stillness that facilitates a faith-filled knowledge of the heart and openness to Jesus. This in turn fans into flame the first love that empowered a personal response in faith. So, returning to the theme of

Jubilee, it is worth exploring the implications for Religious Life in this context.

> Jubilee is healing and joyous, but not sentimental; hard and difficult, yet ultimately a specific, concrete set of responses to the crises of the earth and all who inhabit it. Eventually, Jubilee ushers in an era of forgiveness, freedom, justice and jubilation. It begins, however, with a not-doing: the decision to pause and to let the land lie fallow. It begins in stillness ... that readies us for the next decade, the next century, the next millennium.[3]

How insightful these words are as we reflect on the gift of Religious Life, especially in this Year of Faith. Pope Benedict has invited us to discover afresh the journey of faith so as to shed clearer light on the joy and renewed enthusiasm of encountering Christ. The Letter to the Hebrews gives a very strong message regarding faith and Pope Benedict has outlined this in detail in *Porta Fidei.* He encourages us to keep our gaze fixed on Jesus Christ, the 'pioneer and perfecter of our faith' (Heb12:2): in him all the anguish and all the longing of the human heart finds fulfilment.[4] To keep our gaze on Jesus Christ – this is the crux and the challenge at this moment in history. Religious have always tried to do this but, in this world of unprecedented change, perhaps we need to be reminded that Religious Life is founded on the solid rock of Christ, and God is always drawing us into that exchange of love on which our lives as Religious are founded and grounded.

This message was further emphasised in his homily to Religious on the Feast of Consecrated Life during the Year of Faith. Pope Benedict gives three invitations to

Religious.[5] He urges us to make an inner pilgrimage to rediscover our first love, that moment of recognising the call to radical love when Jesus set our hearts on fire. In this Year of Faith, revisiting the origins of our vocation is a grace to be treasured not only as a precious memory, but as an incentive for an on-going exchange and deepening of love. The very symbolism of fire and fanning into flame is the language of the mystic. It evokes and awakens the yearning for loving union which is the deepest desire of the human heart.

In his second invitation, recognising the values of success and efficiency lauded by our society, Pope Benedict invites us to become an evangelical sign of contradiction. He spells this out by giving the example of the kenosis of Christ who did not cling to his equality with God but assumed the human condition in all its poverty and frailty. Pope Benedict says it is precisely in our limitations and weaknesses as human beings that we are called to live as Christ lived. The invitation to live in humility, lowliness and frailty is at the same time a commitment to solidarity with all our brothers and sisters, especially the poor and the lowly in this world. This is a radical witness to the power of the Paschal Mystery and our participation in this great mystery of our faith, especially in our profession of the evangelical counsels of poverty, chastity and obedience – a point we will develop later.

Lastly, Pope Benedict invites Religious to renew the faith that makes us pilgrims bound for the future. Again, his focus is Christ, the search for the Face that is sometimes revealed and sometimes veiled. The pilgrimage of the spirit in quest of the Absolute will always characterise the yearning heart of the Religious. Everything great and small is guided by this criterion and, with such a criterion as guide, faith is both central and pivotal. Perhaps it is very challenging for us, as Religious, to question whether our faith *is* pivotal in a way that truly guides the great and small events of our lives. Speaking in the context of Consecrated Life, Ruth Burrows says:

> Faith does not get the attention it ought to have. Too often we take it for granted that we have faith and that we live by faith. No doubt this is true in an overall sort of way. But faith, to be real faith, is incessant, always operating, governing the entirety of life, with nothing whatever left out.[6]

Surely this is what Pope Benedict means by the great and small acts in our lives. He is inviting us to be attentive to the place of faith in our lives – the kind of faith that leads to perfect love. He uses the words 'watchful and wakeful'. To ponder this challenge and accept the consequences requires great humility, especially in a world that relativises faith or dismisses it altogether. Therefore, we are called back to gaze on Jesus Christ, the 'pioneer and perfecter of our faith' (Heb 12:2). It is Jesus alone who reveals to us who we are and who God is. There is no other way to understand the call to Religious Life or any other Christian call within the Church. Jesus himself said: 'I am the Way, the Truth and the Life' (Jn 14:6).

With conviction and encouragement, Pope Benedict specifically asks Religious not to join the ranks of the

prophets of doom who proclaim the end or meaningless-
ness of consecrated life in the Church. Rather we are
challenged to clothe ourselves with Christ and radiate
his presence by putting on the armour of light in
watchful, wakeful fidelity. In describing Religious Life,
the theme of Light was beautifully expressed when Pope
Benedict said:

> It shows the beauty and value of the consecrated life as a
> reflection of Christ's light; a sign that recalls Mary's
> entry into the Temple. The Virgin Mary, the Consecrated
> Woman *par excellence*, carried in her arms the Light
> Himself, the Incarnate Word who came to dispel the
> darkness of the world with God's love.[7]

While recognising the joy of the Consecrated Life, Pope
Benedict also points to the reality of the suffering of the
heart, that interior martyrdom that is part and parcel of
being wounded by love. In this we follow the path taken
by Jesus and Mary his Mother. First and foremost this is
a call to become who we are called and destined to
become in and through and with Jesus Christ, the Word
made flesh for love of us. It is the call to be fully human
after the example of Jesus Christ and this involves
growing pains. It means relinquishing everything that
militates against belonging completely and radically to
God. This is not an easy option.

External works, apostolates, ministries of one sort and
another – all of these must first of all be rooted in
steadfast faith in Jesus Christ, who alone reveals
humanity to itself, who alone reveals the Religious to
her/himself. 'If this profound process takes place within
them, they then bear fruit not only in adoration of God

but also in deep wonder at themselves'.[8] The bedrock for this knowledge of God and self is faith. In and through this faith knowledge we are empowered to express the unique and unrepeatable image of the Christ-form in this world. This is how we best serve our sisters and brothers. As the Franciscan scholar, Zachary Hayes has said: each of us is destined to embody something of the Divine Word in our individual lives – not as carbon copies of Jesus or Francis, but to fill the Christ form with the elements of our personal life – in a way unique to us.

After the example of Jesus and Mary, we are invited to witness to evangelical *parrhesia*. Pope Benedict is talking here about biblical confidence or boldness. What an amazing and timely invitation. It is a word that we find in the *Catechism of the Catholic Church* in the section on prayer. Once again, it is the inner pilgrimage, the living relationship of love that expresses itself with great trust, confidence and holy daring in the face of rapid change and challenge. It is the *both/and* experience of shifting sands and solid rock.

Returning to his Apostolic Letter, *Porta Fidei*, Pope Benedict speaks in biblical terms of the desert, saying that this is the time for the Church as a whole to lead the People of God out of the desert towards a place of life. Since the years of Vatican II, Religious Life has also been portrayed in terms of the desert experience. And if forty years symbolises the desert, then fifty years symbolises a time of Jubilee. That is how I would like to present Religious Life at this moment in history, on the fiftieth anniversary of Vatican II. It is a call and an invitation to move to a place of life. In biblical terms Jubilee has two particular and essential characteristics both of which were highlighted by Jesus when he quoted the prophet Isaiah: liberation and consolation.

> The prophet heralds a year of the Lord's favour and not on his own personal initiative, but by means of an unction worked by the Spirit of the Lord: it is a divine gift. And this year expresses itself in two vital, highly positive directions: liberation and consolation. Liberation is from physical evils, from interior lacerations, from the condition of slavery; consolation is a transformation of the way one feels, of the way one exists: from mourning one passes to joy.[9]

Without repeating what has been written in past decades, we can say that there is a real sense in which Religious Life has been liberated from many of the exterior accretions that needed to be discarded in the process of renewal. That said, our focus now is inner liberation from interior lacerations, and also liberation from the condition of slavery. This inner freedom is rooted in the intimacy of indwelling. Jesus said, 'If you make my word your home you will indeed be my disciples; you will come to know the truth, and the truth will set you free' (Jn 8:31–32). The true freedom or liberation promised by Jesus is dependent on intimacy and discipleship, without which true freedom is impossible. Speaking of Catholicism in the twenty-first century, George Weigel argues that 'in the Evangelical Catholicism of the future, deep reform of consecrated life will, like every other facet of authentic Catholic reform, be measured by the twin criteria of truth and mission'.[10]

It would seem therefore, that this Year of Faith is primarily an invitation to deepen our friendship with

Christ, who is the Way, the Truth and the Life, and to enter with wholehearted and loving surrender into his mission for the Church and the world. Jesus alone sets us free, establishes us in the truth of who we are and who he is, and gives life in abundance. The shifting sands of change not only shape and affect us, but they can also throw us back into the arms of God with greater trust and confident boldness, leading to greater love, abandonment and transformation. It is the story of Salvation History. It is the story of the Church. It is the story of Religious Life. It is every person's story.

The Challenge of the Second Vatican Council

At the beginning of the twenty-first century, in his address on the implementation of Vatican II, Pope John Paul II highlighted the Second Vatican Ecumenical Council as being a gift of the Spirit to his Church. In saying this he emphasised the necessity of both understanding the history of the Church and exploring the course of world events in the light of two thousand years of faith, preserved in its original authenticity. He said: 'With the Council, *the Church first had an experience of faith,* as she abandoned herself to God without reserve, as one who trusts and is certain of being loved.'[11] What a wealth of wisdom there is in these words.

Faith, abandonment, trust and love. These are the words of a mystic who is deeply in love with the Mystery in which we are enfolded. These are the words of a man who has a deep grasp of both God and the human condition. And he develops this theme when he

acknowledges that 'What we achieved at the Council
was to show that if contemporary man wants to understand himself completely, he too needs Jesus Christ and
his Church.'[12] Furthermore, the Pope stresses that it
would be a great mistake to interpret the Council on the
supposition that it marks a break with the past, when in
reality it stands in continuity with the faith of all times.
He quotes the words of his predecessor, Pope Paul VI, in
referring to the Council as 'A great, threefold act of love'.
I was very moved by the words in Pope John Paul's
Address and, recognising that Religious Life is at the
very heart of the Church, I wanted to explore the implications of this Address not only for the Church as a
whole but for Religious Life in particular.

A Threefold Act of Love

The Council was 'A great, threefold act of love' – as Pope
Paul VI said in his opening address at the Council's
fourth session – an act of love 'for God, for the Church,
for humanity'. Without historical analysis of past
decades, let us simply take to heart these words as they
relate to the Church and in particular to Religious Life at
the beginning of this twenty-first century. Love is central
without a doubt. That God, the Church and our brothers
and sisters are the focus of this love presents invitations
and challenges that will need to be faced in the context
of faith. In this we are encouraged by the words of Pope
John Paul II:

> What has been believed by 'everyone, always and every-
> where' is the authentic newness that enables every era to

perceive the light that comes from the word of God's
Revelation in Jesus Christ.[13]

Authentic newness! Religious continue to take this to
heart because every individual call from God is an invitation to authentic newness. In the person who is called
by name to the fullness of life and love, God's call gives
shape, identity and form to individual identity and
mission. Received in faith, lived in faith and sustained
by faith, the call to Religious Life constitutes 'a gift of
God which the Church has received from her Lord and
which by his grace she always safeguards'.[14]

Perfectae Caritatis

The document *Perfectae Caritatis* reflects the threefold
act of love referred to above, in that authentic Religious
Life is, and always has been, an act of love for God, for
the Church and for humanity. In a reflection on the
occasion of the fortieth anniversary of *Perfectae
Caritatis*, Archbishop Franc Rodé said, 'No Ecumenical
Council had ever spoken at such length and with such
depth of this important charism in the Church'. In his
view the Council is 'undoubtedly a historical turning
point in theological reflection on the consecrated life'.[15]
Much has been discovered and much has still to be
discovered, a point made by Pope John Paul at the
beginning of this new millennium. 'Only from a faith
perspective can we see the Council event as a gift
whose still hidden wealth we must know how to
mine'.[16] It is our earnest desire to penetrate these
depths and mine the hidden wealth of the Council,

especially as it relates to the precious gift of Religious
Life within the Church.

> The Church first had an experience of faith, as she
> abandoned herself to God without reserve as one who
> trusts and is certain of being loved. It is precisely this act
> of abandonment to God which stands out from an
> objective examination of the Acts (of the Council).
> Anyone who wished to approach the Council without
> considering this interpretive key would be unable to
> penetrate its depths. Only from a faith perspective can
> we see the Council event as a gift whose still hidden
> wealth we must know how to mine.[17]

The two-fold challenge to go back to our sources and to
update our way of life was courageously and wholeheartedly undertaken by Religious Congregations after
Vatican II. The challenges continue to this day. It cannot
be otherwise. As Cardinal John Henry Newman said: 'To
live is to change, and to be perfect is to have changed
often'. This is the human adventure and, as it pertains to
Religious Life, it is wonderful to feel part of a group of
people who take this challenge to heart. While this book
is first and foremost a reflection on the way in which my
own small Congregation has been guided, shaped and
renewed in a discovery and process that is on-going,
there are implications that are relevant to the wider
picture.

I belong to a very small Congregation called Franciscan Sisters Minoress. During this Year of Faith we will
celebrate 125 years of existence. Throughout our history
we have never numbered more than ninety sisters.
Minority or littleness is part of our charism. And in this

respect, I was interested to read the following words by Joan Chittester:

Viability has been computed in terms of numbers far too long, despite the fact that most congregations were started by three of four young women who gave everything they had to work against the odds for something that was impossible to attain. Precisely this emphasis on respect for smallness must prevail again now.[18]

While many Congregations have suffered a very significant decrease in numbers, this has affected us, but not to the extent experienced by some – for smallness has always prevailed. In exploring our charism of minority, we have been led in amazing ways to a deeper identification with Christ and our Gospel way of life. This is a point I will develop further in another chapter. My intention here is to mention the importance of returning to the sources, the founding charism, and this was a clarion call from Vatican II.

When Pope John Paul called the Synod in 1994, it was to consider the state and reform of Consecrated Life within the Church, especially since the years of Vatican II. Following the Synod, Pope John Paul issued a seminal document in 1996 entitled *Vita Consecrata*. As a Congregation, this Document came at a time when we were preparing for our General Chapter which was due in 1997. For a whole year this was a key Document for us as we studied, reflected and cherished its contents, challenges and teachings. Following our Chapter we felt empowered to try to put into practice what had become a blueprint for renewal and reform at both a personal and Congregational level. The consequences of this will be filtered through the following chapters.

Vita Consecrata

What would become of the world if there were no Religious? This was the question posed by Pope John Paul II in *Vita Consecrata*. He questioned the value of Religious Life beyond superficial assessments of its usefulness and came to the conclusion that unbounded generosity and love were essential in this particular form of Christian witness in the Church and the world. Quoting Pope Paul VI, he said:

> Without this concrete sign there would be a danger that the charity that animates the entire Church would grow cold, that the salvific paradox of the Gospel would be blunted, and that the 'salt' of faith would lose its savour in a world undergoing secularization.[19]

This is an amazing statement. It takes us right back to St Paul's conviction in his Letter to the Corinthians. We are all familiar with this text, so familiar that perhaps we take it for granted or allow it to grow dull as it applies to our particular way of life. It was this text that fired the heart of Thérèse of Lisieux and gave purpose and meaning to every moment of her enclosed Carmelite life. She was love within the Church. She realised that the Church needs a heart burning and beating with love. Yes, as St Paul says:

> If I speak in the tongues of men and of angels, but have not love, I am a noisy gong or a clanging symbol. And if

I have prophetic powers, and understand all mysteries and all knowledge, and if I have all faith, so as to remove mountains, but have not love, I am nothing. If I give away all I have, and if I deliver my body to be burned, but have not love, I gain nothing.

(1 Cor 13:1–3)

We Religious have not been silent in recent decades. We have made a noise within the Church and the world. We have highlighted and at times reclaimed our prophetic stance within the Church. We have persevered in great faith, removing mountains of obstacles and useless accretions associated with our way of life. We have desired to give away all that we are and all that we have for love of God and our brothers and sisters. In some cases many of our brothers and sisters have given their lives as martyrs. And St Paul reminds us that the primacy in all of these things is love. That is my emphasis too in this reflection, desiring that we will continue to abandon our lives, in a continuous crescendo, into the hands of Love made flesh in Jesus Christ. The handing over of ourselves to Jesus Christ, will affect our lifestyle, our ministries and our spirituality. This is what a return to the sources and an updating really involves. It is a journey into the heart of God for the increase of holiness in the Church, for the greater glory of God who is the source and origin of all holiness, and for the life of the world.

In *Lumen Gentium* the chapter on *Religious* follows immediately after the chapter on *The Call to Holiness*. 'All the members of the Church should unflagingly fulfil the duties of their Christian calling. The profession of the evangelical counsels shines before them as a sign which can and should effectively inspire them to do so'.[20] Again in 1996, Pope John Paul II reiterates the same truth, saying that a renewed commitment to holiness by consecrated Religious is more necessary than ever. To the degree that this happens within the heart of the consecrated Religious, to that extent are we prepared to help our brothers and sisters in their search for God and the courageous and sometimes heroic demands faith makes on them. 'Consecrated persons at the deepest level of their being are caught up in the dynamism of the Church's life, which is thirsty for the divine Absolute and called to holiness. It is to this holiness that they bear witness'.[21]

The call to be a Religious is a divine call. It is an invitation to give expression to the unique vocation that shapes and forms the human person. Faith is very important here because Scripture tells us that 'Before I formed you in the womb, I knew you' (Jer 1:4). What an amazing truth! From all eternity, even before our entry into our mother's womb you and I are in the heart of God. 'The claim of our faith is that every human life is a response to a summons from God to share the life of the Trinity'.[22] Father Timothy Radcliffe goes on to say that this summons is to life. Therefore, personal identity is a gift, and the story of my life and yours is made up of all those choices to accept or refuse that gift. He refers to Paul's Letter to the Corinthians, 'It is God who has called you to share in the life of his Son, Jesus Christ our Lord; and God keeps faith (1 Cor 1:9).

For the person called to Religious Life, it is a particular and radical way of saying 'Yes' to that call to life.

Jesus said: 'I have come that they may have life and have it to the full' (Jn 10:10). Religious mirror back to every person his or her unique call and destiny to share in the very life of God. In a society that does not always value life from conception to birth, Religious have a very real challenge to witness to the unique and precious gift of every human life with its particular and potential call and response. *Perfectae Caritatis* goes on to explain that fidelity to the charism of the Institute is a powerful way to make Christ present in an unbelieving world. This is a point to which we will return in a later chapter.

Within the call to holiness is a witness to the life of communion. Pope John Paul II describes consecrated persons as 'true experts of communion' which becomes for the whole world 'a sign and a compelling force to faith in Christ'.[23] Today in the Third Millennium, the challenging words of *Vita Consecrata* resound with urgency as we participate in the New Evangelisation. Pope John Paul II envisaged consecrated persons contributing to elaborating and putting into effect new initiatives of evangelisation for present day situations. He says, 'All this will be done in the certainty of faith that the Spirit can give satisfactory replies even to the most difficult questions'.[24] And the perennial question is: Who am I?

Authors speak of a crisis of faith and a crisis of identity. Both seem to be closely related, and Religious have also been affected by both crises. After all, the people who enter Religious Life have been shaped by the world around them and the world as we know it has certainly suffered from a crisis of faith and a crisis of identity. Perhaps this is why the document *Starting*

Afresh from Christ[25] emphasises the role of faith in consecrated life in the Third Millennium.

Starting Afresh from Christ

Published in 2002, this document refers to faith and
faithfulness with great insistence and emphasis, noting
its place, contribution and witness in the life of consecrated persons. Right at the beginning we read:
'Consecrated persons must seek a new impetus in
Christian living, making it the force which inspires their
journey of faith'.[26] Newness and faith: two realities we
have already highlighted so that, with the Apostle Paul,
it is possible to say: 'I still live my human life, but it is a
life of faith in the Son of God who loved *me* and gave his
life for *me*'.[27]

The document further emphasises that, with a vision
of faith, even negative experiences can be the occasion
for a new beginning. This must sound both familiar and
reassuring to many Religious Congregations, given their
experiences during past decades. However, this is not a
reality that is peculiar to Religious. 'Consecrated
persons are not alone in living the tension between secu-
larism and an authentic life of faith, between the
fragility of humanity itself and the power of grace; this is
the experience of all members of the Church'.[28] Without
repeating what many authors have written about the
challenges and changes in our Church and our world,
and the way in which these have impacted Religious
Life, perhaps our present focus on faith and love invites
us to reclaim and recover our lost confidence in our
unique and personal call from God. To the extent that we

do this, we will impart to every human being a sense of his or her personal vocation. To develop a culture of vocation is one of the present day challenges, but it is rooted in understanding the dignity of the human person, uniquely created in the image and likeness of God.

God loves each one of us into life, gifting us with the capacity for self-determination and freedom. The only way to become the person God created us to be is to respond wholeheartedly to our personal vocation. Religious choose to respond to God's initiative in embracing a life of consecration through the evangelical counsels of poverty, chastity and obedience. This is a gift to be received in faith from the Love that is within the Trinity. It is a gift to be lived in joyful trust and confident boldness. It is a gift to be renewed each day. It is a gift not only for the person called but also for the Church and the world.

Reflection

In what ways do you see the vocation to Religious Life as a radical and daring adventure in love, offered to individuals as a unique and personal call from God?

Notes

1 Pope Benedict XVI, *Porta Fidei*, 7.
2 J. Chittister, OSB, *The Fire In These Ashes, A Spirituality of Contemporary Religious Life.* Leominister: Gracewing, 1995, p. viii.
3 M. Harris, *Proclaim Jubilee A Spirituality for the Twenty-First Century.* Kentucky: Westminster John Knox Press, 1996, p. 16.
4 Pope Benedict XVI, *Porta Fidei*, 13.

5 Pope Benedict, Homily, 2 February 2013.
6 R. Burrows, OCD, *Essence of Prayer*. London: Burns & Oates, 2006, p. 198.
7 Pope Benedict, Homily, 2 February 2013.
8 Pope John Paul II, *Redemptoris Hominis*, 10.
9 L. Pacomio, *Jubilee in the Bible*. Vatican Publications, 2000.
10 G. Weigel, *Evangelical Catholicism, Deep Reform in the Twenty-First Century Church*. NY: Basic Books, 2013, p. 188.
11 Pope John Paul II, *Address to the Conference Studying the Implementation of the Second Vatican Council*. Rome, 2000.
12 Ibid.
13 Ibid.
14 A. Flannery, OP, *Vatican Council II The Conciliar and Post Conciliar Documents*. Leominster: Fowler Wright Books Ltd, 1981, *Lumen Gentium*, 43.
15 Archbishop Franc Rodé, *Reflection on Occasion of the 40th Anniversary of Perfectae Caritatis*, p. 1.
16 Ibid., 2.
17 Ibid., 2.
18 J. Chittester, Article in *Catholic Reporter*, 1994.
19 Pope John Paul II, *Vita Consecrata*, 105.
20 A. Flannery, OP, *Vatican Council II The Conciliar and Post Conciliar Documents, Lumen Gentium*, 44.
21 Pope John Paul II, *Vita Consecrata*, 39
22 T. Radcliffe, *Keynote Address to the U.S. Conference of Major Superiors for Men* (CMSM), 1996.
23 Pope John Paul II, *Vita Consecrata*, 46.
24 Ibid., 73.
25 Congregation for Institutes of Consecrated Life and Societies of Apostolic Life, Instruction, *Starting Afresh from Christ: A Renewed Commitment to Consecrated Life in the Third Millennium*. London: CTS, 2002.
26 Ibid., p. 2.
27 Ibid., p. 5.
28 Ibid., p. 15.

Chapter Two

Radical Gift

*In every age, the Spirit enables new men and women to
recognise the appeal of such a demanding choice.*

(Vita Consecrata, 19)

Radical gift! These words are our starting point. The
evangelical counsels are considered 'a divine gift that
the Church has received from its Lord', in such a way
that Religious Life which is organized around them,
appears in its totality as a 'special gift, from God to his
Church, so that it can accomplish its saving mission'.[1] In
the profession of the evangelical counsels, this precious
gift is received in faith and responded to in faith, making
Religious a kind of sign and prophetic statement. The
Second Vatican Council did not refer specifically to
Religious Life as a charism but it did recognise the
charismatic dimension of Religious Life.

Vita Consecrata leaves us in no doubt regarding the
radical and gifted nature of consecrated life. It is first
and foremost a gift of the Holy Spirit and this is spelled
out in great detail throughout the document. Using the
great love theme of Sacred Scripture, 'You have seduced
me, Lord, and I have let myself be seduced' (Jer 20:7), we
are led into a profound reflection on the way in which
the recipient of this love responds. Always it is the

working of the Holy Spirit in awakening the desire to respond fully to this overture of love. It is the Holy Spirit who guides and inspires the growth and response in love, empowering and sustaining the faith of the one called. Again under the influence of the same Holy Spirit, the heart of the person called to this vocation is shaped and moulded towards maturity in a grace that configures us to Christ, poor, chaste and obedient.

To enable us to enter more deeply into our vocation, in *Vita Consecrata* Pope John Paul II highlights several significant Scripture texts in which Religious are challenged to greater faith and love in radical identification with Christ. These are the Transfiguration, the story of Martha and Mary, the anointing at Bethany and the example of Our Blessed Lady at the foot of the Cross and in the Upper Room. We will look at these in turn and glean from them the riches that will make Religious Life in the twenty-first century alive with the Spirit, and fruitful for the mission of the Church and the world.

The Transfiguration

The evangelical basis of consecrated life is the special relationship the person called has with Jesus. We are left in no doubt that 'the evangelical basis of consecrated life is to be sought in the special relationship which Jesus, in his earthly life, established with some of his disciples'.[2] And Pope John Paul invites Religious to a deeper understanding of our call and vocation by gazing on the face of Christ in the mystery of the Transfiguration. This is an overriding theme of *Vita Consecrata*. The choice of this event from Sacred Scripture is profoundly insightful.

There is special mention of the bright cloud that over-shadowed the apostles during the Transfiguration. While this is symbolic of the presence of the Holy Spirit, the very paradox of 'bright cloud' suggests that the radiant, inner reality is hidden or clouded within the ordinary, but is transfigured by faith. 'Only faith can guarantee the blessings that we hope for, or prove the existence of realities that are unseen' (Heb 11:1). And in this Year of Faith this theme will weave through our reflections on Consecrated Life.

In choosing the event of the Transfiguration to elucidate the call to Consecrated Life, Pope John Paul II beautifully and powerfully challenges Religious to recognise the essence of our call to love. Mountains are the favoured meeting places with God. Therefore, going up the mountain with Jesus is essentially a call to contemplative prayer, intimacy and love. The history of Christian spirituality teaches us that there is what we might call 'mountain symbolism' at the heart of our tradition. The mountain in Sacred Scripture and in the mystical tradition symbolises the transcendence of God and our approach and response in love and adoration. Just as mystics and psychologists speak of mountain peaks, don't we too speak symbolically of 'peak moments' in our lives?

More often than not, a mountain peak is 'veiled' in mist or cloud. So too, in our 'peak experiences' in prayer, we may be given a glimpse of something of the transcendence and glory of God, though in a veiled manner. In Sacred Scripture, the glory of God is often manifested in the form of a cloud, or a fire, or with thunder and lightning. It seems that the experience of the transcen-

dent God is so overwhelming that a cloud covers the
presence of God to some extent, so that we poor humans
are protected from the full reality and force of that
presence. We see this with the apostles at the Transfiguration on Mount Tabor.

St Gregory of Nyssa, compares the knowledge of God
to a mountain steep to climb, intimating that the person
who desires to associate intimately with God must go
beyond all that is visible, as to a mountaintop and
encounter, to the invisible and incomprehensible. The
personal encounter in faith is essential, inviting radical
openness and receptivity. It is God who takes the initiative. It is God who leads us to this deeper experience of
our personal call. Like any love relationship we are
invited into new levels of relationship with God. Part of
this experience means that our usual ways of seeing and
knowing no longer help us. It may feel like alien
territory as the Mount Tabor experience did to the
apostles. Yet in the midst of this new experience, there is
the personal encounter that is central and essential for
deeper union in radical self-giving and configuration
with Christ. But, in the intimacy enjoyed in the presence
of Christ and the splendour and glory of life within the
Trinity, there is also the call to embrace the Cross in total,
self-giving love and service to our brothers and sisters.
'Let the Cross be for you, as it was for Christ, proof of the
greatest love. Is there not a mysterious relationship
between renunciation and joy, between sacrifice
and magnanimity, between discipline and spiritual
freedom?'[3] As Jesus said to his first followers, 'If anyone
wants to be a follower of mine, let him renounce himself
and take up his cross and follow me. Anyone who wants

to save his life will lose it; but anyone who loses his life for my sake will find it' (Mt 16:24–25). That is the paradox of radical Gospel living to which Religious are personally called.

Like Peter, James and John, we are called to gaze upon the face of Christ radiant in glory, for 'by the profession of the evangelical counsels the characteristic features of Jesus – the chaste, poor and obedient one – are made constantly 'visible' in the midst of the world'. At the same time 'Religious have helped to make the mystery and mission of the Church shine forth, and in doing so have contributed to the renewal of society'.[4] There is a wealth of teaching and challenge in these words. The challenge to proclaim Christ's glory and reveal his features in the midst of the world. I am in awe of the privilege of such a call and vocation. Like the apostles, to live it fully requires spending time *on* the mountain but also returning *from* the mountain.

The Transfiguration is a decisive moment in the ministry of Jesus. Significantly, as St Luke points out, this experience happened while Jesus was at prayer, and what happened to him will happen to us if we too are faithful to prayer. 'As he was praying, the aspect of his face was changed' (Lk 9:29). As one author eloquently says: 'Transfiguration means that our authentic, original beauty shines through. God's radiance, which is in us, shines from our face. We recognise that we are the glory of God'.[5] This is another way of saying that each of us has a personal vocation, a way of expressing the Christ-form in us that is absolutely unrepeatable and unique. For those called to Religious Life, there is a particular challenge posed in *Vita Consecrata* that is captured in the story of the Transfiguration, hence the need to ponder and pray with this text to unpack its riches.

Like the apostles, this revelatory event strengthens our faith too, especially in the mystery of the face of Jesus, transfigured in glory and disfigured on the Cross. In the embrace of both, we share in the Christ Mystery and somehow hold them together in a way that expresses the radical nature of Religious Life. 'All are equally called to follow Christ ... but those who are called to the consecrated life have a special experience of the light which shines from the Incarnate Word'.[6] Making Jesus the focus of loving communion, we are caught up in his splendour, listening to him, trusting in him and making him the centre of our lives. In so doing we are engaged in the prolongation in history of a special presence of the Risen Lord. Making visible the characteristic features of Jesus and helping to make the mystery and mission of the Church shine forth are profound realities. But we are assured that 'In every age, the Spirit enables new men and women to recognise the appeal of such a demanding choice'.[7] While every Christian is called to make visible the characteristic features of Jesus, Religious, through a vowed life of poverty, chastity and obedience, do this in a specific way through the charism of their Institutes. This is a tremendous privilege with far-reaching consequences and we will develop the gift of different charisms in our next chapter.

I was intrigued by Pope John Paul II's choice of the story of the Transfiguration as a model for understanding Religious Life. This led me to do a little research on the meaning of transfiguration and how it differed from transformation. Certainly the Gospel accounts speak of Jesus being transfigured, so I began to explore what this process meant for Jesus, for the apostles who witnessed the event, and for Religious today. I soon realised I was in the realm of deep mystery and grace. Transfiguration is an act of God because it is an act of revelation. God allows human beings, in this case Peter, James and John, to behold the glory of Jesus. Transfiguration did not change Jesus – the divine and human second Person of the Blessed Trinity – it just revealed what was not always apparent to those who beheld him in his humanity. In this wonderful and mysterious event on Mount Tabor the apostles were allowed to glimpse, here on earth, something of the glory of Jesus. He was still the same person who walked and talked with them on the plain. They saw only the outward appearance change: his face and his clothing. Both radiated the inner light that was always within him.

We are made in God's image and likeness but, unlike Jesus, we do not have the same fullness of life and love as he does. This is where the challenge comes. We are called to transformation so that the life of Christ will be allowed to shine through in varying degrees as we grow from glory to glory in union with him. This requires our freedom and co-operation so that eventually, through our free co-operation with divine grace, we too will be transfigured as we share in his life and love within the Blessed Trinity.

Many references in the Letters of St Paul help us to realise the depth and meaning of what it means to be transformed – even in this life – from glory to glory. 'All of us, with our unveiled faces like mirrors, reflecting the glory of the Lord, are being transformed into the image that we reflect in brighter and brighter glory; this is the work of the Lord who is the Spirit' (2 Cor 3:18). And in Colossians we read: 'It was God's purpose to reveal to them how rich is the glory of this mystery … it is Christ among you, your hope of glory' (Col 1:27). Here we are in the realm of inscrutable mystery and Saint John Paul II invites us to enter this mystery in a special way through the evangelical counsels of poverty, chastity and obedience as consecrated Religious.

The challenges presented in the story of the Transfiguration are not a once and for all experience, but an on-going invitation to greater identity and union with Christ. This call to intimacy and union is revealed especially in those moments of personal prayer and contemplation, which are of the essence of Religious Life. 'The path which consecrated life is called to take up at the beginning of the new millennium is guided by the contemplation of Christ with a gaze fixed, more than ever, on the face of the Lord'.[8] As this *Instruction* points out, Religious are challenged to discover the face of Christ in a multiplicity of presences in ways that are ever new. Religious have always tried to do this but it is interesting that the focus is the contemplation of the face of Christ which requires deep faith and love, especially in the light of the charism of each particular Religious family.

The Anointing at Bethany

One contemporary writer points out that *Vita Consecrata* is a charter for the reform of Religious Life in the twenty-first century.[9] He also points out that the other biblical vignettes used by Pope John Paul II illustrate crucial aspects of the consecrated life as a life transformed in the on going encounter with the Transfigured Lord and his glory. We will now turn briefly to those biblical stories and unpack their riches in relation to our theme of radical gift and on-going encounter. Let us turn first to the story of the Anointing at Bethany. Then as now, what happened in Bethany continues to raise questions of meaning and relevance. And as Pope John Paul II points out, the questions raised today spring from our 'utilitarian and technocratic culture which is inclined to assess the importance of things and even of people in relation to their immediate "usefulness" '.[10] This is very evident in the story of The Anointing at Bethany (Jn 12:1–11). The story is familiar and it has special significance for Religious. Pondering on Mary anointing the feet of Jesus with very precious and expensive perfume, pure nard, denotes an act of pure love and costly service 'that transcends all "utilitarian" considerations, it is a sign of unbounded generosity ... From such a life "poured out" without reserve there spreads a fragrance which fills the whole house'.[11] Here, the whole house refers to the Church. So, what is the significance of the Anointing at Bethany for Religious today? Why did Pope John Paul II highlight this story in *Vita Consecrata*?

To answer this question, perhaps we need to look carefully at the different groups mentioned in this story. Jesus is there and in his presence we have Martha, Lazarus, Mary, the apostles and a large number who came to the house because they were curious. Straight away we are told that Martha waited on them at table.

There is a time and a place for loving service and there is a time for intensely focusing on the Lord himself. What is highlighted in this scene is Mary's total attention on the Person of Jesus. She seems to have an inner grasp of his mission, especially the meaning of his saving death as the greatest act of self-giving and sacrificial love. She who sat at his feet had listened well. Her heart understood and her response was, like his, extravagant and reckless, as love's expression often is. It would seem that the apostles had not reached this depth of understanding of God's self-giving and extravagant love in the Incarnate Jesus; but they, like us, would eventually grow into a love that was willing to lay down life for love of him. 'No one can have greater love than to lay down his life for his friends' (Jn 15:13). Those who had gathered at the house for reasons of curiosity, especially following the sensational raising of Lazarus from the dead, also had a long way to go in their relationship with Jesus, but it often happens that curiosity – for whatever reasons – often leads to the truth.

Our lives as Religious, at different moments, reflect the loving service of Martha, the extravagant love of Mary, the misunderstanding of the apostles, especially when the Martha/Mary dilemma of prayer versus service becomes *either/or* rather than *both/and*. We will return to this delicate point when we develop our chapter on the special charisms that characterise each Religious Institute. Like the scene at Bethany, our lives of consecration sometimes draw the attention of those who are curious or seeking answers. But for Pope John Paul II, the most significant aspect of the Bethany episode for Religious is the absolute relevance of a life of

radical love and unbounded generosity. In highlighting
the person of Mary, we see straight away that unless we
are deeply rooted in a very personal relationship with
Christ, taking time to gaze on his face in contemplation,
captivated by his love and goodness and his beauty and
glory, we will run the risk of becoming disillusioned,
questioning the usefulness of our lives in a world that
seems at times to reflect the attitudes and behaviours of
others who were present at the dinner table in Bethany.

The Example of Mary the Mother of Jesus

We now turn our attention to another Mary, the Mother of
Jesus. *Vita Consecrata* highlights the example of Mary as
the perfect disciple. From the Annunciation when we first
hear of Mary, until Pentecost when we last hear of her,
Mary is the 'sublime example of perfect consecration'.[12]
In her total belonging to God and devotion to him, Mary
is a constant reminder to us of the primacy of God's initiative. From my long involvement in the ministry of
formation and vocation discernment, I am acutely aware
that this aspect of call and vocation takes time to process
and mature. Oftentimes in the self-absorption of God-
given freedom, some discerners tend to think everything
depends on them! Time and prayerful reflection lead to a
much more exciting, exhilarating and humbling experience of the very personal love of the One who takes the
initiative and awaits a personal response. In this very
personal relationship of call and response, Mary is 'the
model of the acceptance of grace'.[13]

   Vita Consecrata presents just four events in Mary's life
– the Annunciation, the Visitation, Calvary and the

Upper Room at Pentecost – as very pertinent for Religious. I would like to look briefly at these moments and see what message we can glean that encourages, inspires, supports and challenges us in our lives as twenty-first century Religious.

The beautiful and memorable words of Mary in St Luke's Gospel, 'Behold, I am the handmaid of the Lord; let it be done to me according to your word' (Lk 1:38), reveal Mary's attitude of total and unconditional self-surrender to the plan of God. Willingly she puts herself at the service of God's plan by the total gift of self for the whole of humanity.

This mirrors the total surrender and radical self-gift of Religious in professing the evangelical counsels. Accepting the primacy of God's initiative and placing ourselves at the service of his plan, we embrace the gift of the evangelical counsels as a way of surrendering to the Lord. In so doing we are called to make visible the marvels wrought by God in our frail humanity. By a radical living out of our consecration, we are called to witness to a transfigured life capable of amazing the world. We will not delve in detail into a study of the three vows of poverty, chastity and obedience. There are already many scholarly works in this area. Suffice it to say that in and through the gift of the evangelical counsels, Religious respond to the infinite love of the Trinity with a total and unconditional gift of self, to be at the disposal of God and his plan for the world, just as Mary was at the Annunciation.

Pope John Paul II also entrusts Religious to the Virgin of the Visitation that, like Mary, we might go forth to meet human needs, but above all bring Jesus to our brothers and sisters. The call is to proclaim and extol the greatness of God and glorify his Name. In the next chapter when we look at different models of Religious Life, the Annunciation and the Visitation will be particularly significant; therefore we will not develop their significance at this point but simply point to the proclamation of God's goodness and greatness and to the aspect of service which are distinguishing characteristics of the vowed life.

Mary at the foot of the Cross on Calvary is central to understanding the spiritual motherhood to which Religious are called. When Jesus said, 'Woman, this is your son', then to the disciple, 'This is your mother' (Jn 19:27), Mary accepted her spiritual motherhood for all time. The Fathers of the Church emphasised her spiritual motherhood in their writings and that same reality is emphasised once again in *Vita Consecrata*. 'The consecrated life has always been seen primarily in terms of Mary – Virgin and Bride. This virginal love is the source of a particular fruitfulness which fosters the birth and growth of divine life in people's hearts'.[14]

As *Vita Consecrata* points out: 'In the consecrated life, particular importance attaches to the spousal meaning'[15] and in this context the example is given of Mary in prayerful expectation in the Upper Room, awaiting the Holy Spirit. Mary – Virgin, Bride and Mother – is our model of fruitfulness in the Church. I am focusing on this spousal love because for me it has been central to understanding of my own vocation to Religious Life. This reality has changed and grown with me over the years but it is still as vibrant and meaningful for me today as it was at the outset of my vocation. While this metaphor may not speak to everyone, it still continues to help some Religious in understanding their call and vocation, uniting as it does the two great command-ments of love – love of God and love of neighbour. In this sense spousal love is 'on the one hand passionately personal and exclusive and on the other hand all-embracing and inclusive'.[16]

The Franciscan Experience

In our Franciscan Tradition spiritual motherhood is central in the lives and writings of both St Francis and St Clare, and is later developed by St Bonaventure. Mystics as they were, it is not surprising that they would pay particular attention to spiritual motherhood, a natural consequence of mystical espousal to Christ, as I have pointed out elsewhere:

> The whole concept of spousal love is a tremendously demanding and challenging one. It presupposes a union with the beloved not only in joy and happiness but also in poverty, humility and crucified love that is inherent in transformation and in unconditional and self-giving service to one's brothers and sisters.[17]

In the lives of Francis and Clare, and indeed in our lives as Religious, spousal love is not a mere romantic or sentimental notion. The demands and challenges are very real because true love is costly if embraced totally on a daily basis, lived in community and in service to the creation of authentic sister/brotherhood. St Francis in his *Second Letter to the Faithful*, writes in deeply relational and spousal language about spiritual motherhood, not just for Religious but for all the faithful.

> We are spouses when the faithful soul is joined by the Holy Spirit to our Lord Jesus Christ. We are brothers, moreover, when we do the will of His Father who is in Heaven; mothers when we carry Him in our heart and body through love and a pure and sincere conscience; ... O how holy, consoling to have such a such a beautiful and wonderful Spouse.[18]

It is obvious that the mystery of Grace is rooted in relationship. From the moment of Baptism when we are plunged into the life of the Trinity and enter into filial, fraternal and spousal relationships with the Three Divine Persons, these relationships develop in intensity according to the call and vocation of each person. As a Franciscan I am very attracted to the specific self-understanding of St Clare as Spouse, Mother and Sister. In her very first Letter to Agnes of Prague, Clare refers to these relationships, saying, 'You are the spouse and the mother and the sister of my Lord Jesus Christ'.[19] I do not think we can separate these realities, and for me they resonate with my own experience of many years in Franciscan Religious Life. Therefore, I would like to dwell briefly on these three relationships with special reference to the writings of Saint Clare.

Clare as Spouse

In the opinion of one contemporary author, 'The modern mind finds little difficulty with the titles of mother and sister. But we find it strange to see a life dedicated to

God as that of a bride'.[20] The author suggests that the
difficulty may have arisen because of the 'cloying senti-
mentality' that obscured the deepest sense of the word.
The term 'Bride of Christ', inspired my response to my
Religious vocation, and it has continued to inspire and
challenge me as my understanding has deepened and
matured over the years. For me it is fundamental in my
relationship with Christ. Perhaps that is one of the
reasons why I am so attracted to Clare's self-understanding as Spouse of Christ.

From her Letters to Agnes of Prague, we can see how
very fundamental the mystical spousal relationship with
Christ was for St Clare. Obviously she was imbued with
scriptural texts such as the Song of Songs and the
Psalms, especially Psalm forty-five which celebrates a
royal wedding, St Paul's Letter to the Corinthians and
the Office of St Agnes which has many references to the
spousal relationship of the consecrated virgin with her
Lord. I can well remember at my Reception ceremony as
a novice, I had to repeat the words: 'I am espoused to
Him Whom Angels serve'. These words are taken
directly from the Office of St Agnes with which Clare
would have been familiar, evident from her use of them
in her Letter to Agnes of Prague. However, it has been
pointed out that Clare is also very much aware of being
a humble servant and handmaiden of her Lord Jesus
Christ. He is always her Lord as well as her Spouse.
Though her 'intimate relationship to the Lord confers a
special dignity ... she can never see herself on the same
level'.[21] Clare's awareness of being a Spouse does not
lessen her awareness of being a handmaid of the Lord.
What matters to Clare is loving union with her Beloved,

sharing his life, his love and his mission in service to his brothers and sisters. Quoting the Song of Songs, Clare writes, 'Draw me after You! We will run in the fragrance of Your perfumes'.[22] There are many commentaries on the Song of Songs and one interpretation of these lines suggests allusions to the active and contemplative aspects of every vocation: being *drawn* into intimacy and *running* in service to one's brothers and sisters. This is where the Bride image gives way to the fruitfulness of motherhood, the normal consequence of the Bride-Bridegroom relationship, whether physical or spiritual. 'For one can be a mother and sister to any number of persons, but a bride to only one'.[23] As mentioned above, this single-hearted devotion and apostolic fruitfulness is emphasised in *Vita Consecrata* when speaking of the example of the Blessed Virgin Mary. Therefore, with Mary as her inspiration and model, let us see how Clare, and each of us, is called to an exclusive love relationship with Christ the Bridegroom, which in turn reaches out to all our brothers and sisters with an all-embracing and inclusive love, making us a mother and sister to all.

Clare as Mother

In her 'Third Letter to Agnes of Prague', Clare writes: 'Therefore, as the glorious Virgin of virgins, carried Christ materially in her body, you too, by following in His footprints (cf. 1 Pet 2:21), especially those of poverty and humility, can, without any doubt, always carry Him spiritually in your chaste and virginal body'.[24] In writing this, Clare understood at a deep level that this is what has taken place at the Incarnation. It is much more than an historical event. It is in fact a call to motherhood for every person and for all time. In her writings she spells out the details of this spiritual motherhood and what it involves on a day-to-day basis. For Clare, spiritual motherhood is deeply rooted in a loving, tender, compassionate nurturing of life, sometimes expressed in hidden and humble service and at other times in miraculous healings. Down-to-earth necessity prompted the motherly response of Clare towards her sisters, Francis and his brothers, and to the local people of Assisi. All recognised in her the solicitude and tender love of one who radiates the feminine face of God as she imitates the example of the Blessed Virgin Mary.

According to one Franciscan scholar, 'there are three areas in which human life needs the feminine activity of nurturing: the body, the heart and the spirit'.[25] Godet develops these areas in the context of relationships. The body is the primary means of communication in interpersonal relationships, hence Clare's appreciation of meeting its needs in order to be an effective instrument. For Clare the heart is the seat of tenderness, and with great love and sensitivity she shares her feelings about the source of such tenderness and love, her Spouse, Jesus Christ. This love and tenderness led Clare to nurture, not just the bodies and emotional lives of those whose lives she touched, but as teacher and mentor, to nurture the life of the spirit, and inspire others to seek the things that really matter. In these ways Clare nurtured life, that gift from the Source of Life who came so that we might have life and live it to the full.

Undoubtedly, Clare cherished the privilege and challenge of spiritual motherhood.

Her example and inspiration was the Blessed Virgin Mary, the servant and handmaid of the Lord. For Our Lady and for St Clare, motherhood means being a servant and 'a co-worker with God ... a support of the weak members of His ineffable Body.'[26] In the *Bull of Canonisation*, it was said of Clare, 'The more she broke the alabaster jar of her body ... the more did the perfume of her holiness spread throughout the whole Church'. Here we can see a direct link with the beautiful biblical story of the Anointing at Bethany, outlined in *Vita Consecrata*, and presented as a model for apostolic effectiveness in the Church and the world. I would now like to turn to Clare as Sister.

Clare as Sister

At the very heart of the Franciscan Movement is the call to be sister and brother to all. In this Francis and Clare excelled. From the written accounts of those who lived with Clare, we gather that being a sister to all was extremely important to her. She received her sisters as gifts given to her from the Lord. Consequently, there was no superiority, domination or authoritarian attitude in Clare's lived experience in community. She chose the way of sisterhood, expressing love and tenderness, respect and mutuality, service and acceptance, accountability and co-responsibility. These are evident from her *Letters*, her *Rule*, her *Testament* and from those whose words are recorded in the *Bull of Canonisation*. Each sister is therefore called to live radically the two great commandments of love, the bedrock of authentic Christian living. Clare in her *Testament* states:

Loving one another with the charity of Christ, let the
love you have in your hearts be shown outwardly in
your deeds so that, compelled by such an example, the
sisters may always grow in love of God and in charity
for one another'.[27]

Clare created an atmosphere where each sister could
grow in closer union with God and with others. Her
understanding of Religious Life was very different from
other models at that time. Hers was a vision of Franciscan evangelical life as lived and mirrored in the life of St
Francis. Living as sisters was not confined to her
community at San Damiano. Clare realised the univer-
sality of her mission. 'For the Lord Himself not only has
set us as an example and mirror for others, but also for
our own sisters whom the Lord has called to our way of
life, so that they in turn will be a mirror and example to
those living in the world'.[28]

Clare fully understood that she and her sisters could be
mirrors for others only if they first of all gazed into the
Mirror which is Christ. This, for her, is the content and
meaning of contemplative prayer, which becomes the
means of personal transformation in Christ. Clare is so
convinced of this that she writes to Agnes of Prague in
these words: 'Transform your whole being into the image
of the Godhead Itself through contemplation'.[29] This
amazing insight captures the essence of the spiritual
journey into the Heart of God Who is love, because it is
the power of love that transforms. How well Clare would
have understood the twofold challenge of *Vita Consecrata*:
transformation through transfiguration. Simply by
gazing at the Mirror, Who is Christ, we are changed into

his image and likeness. But we have to be there, in his Presence for transformation to happen.

Just as *Vita Consecrata* and *Starting Afresh from Christ*, state that it is singularly helpful to fix our gaze on the radiant face of Christ, so too, Clare emphasises the necessity of doing likewise. 'Gaze upon Him, consider Him, contemplate Him, as you desire to imitate Him'.[30] There is no other way to meet the challenge of revealing the face of Jesus to the world. Through daily gazing into the face of Christ, the Mirror, we begin to discover his reflection in ourselves. This leads to union and transformation in such a way that others begin to see the face of God in us. For Clare, contemplation leads to imitation but each of us is called to reflect that face in a way that is absolutely unique and unrepeatable. 'In every person, no-one excluded, there is an original gift of God which waits to be discovered'.[31] What an awesome privilege and perennial challenge for every person. How fortunate we are to have saints whose personal examples give us help, advice, encouragement and inspiration for the journey.

Francis and Clare made a tremendous difference to the Church and the world of the thirteenth century, especially in the newness they brought to Religious Life. Both spoke of our relationship as spouses, mothers and brothers of Our Lord Jesus Christ. Such relationships are steeped in the mystery of the Incarnation. 'A relationship with Christ as the Word-made-flesh also defines one's relationship to all the members of His body'.[32] Again, the two great Commandments to love are central. The examples of Francis and Clare continue to impact and inspire, and in view of the reflections in this chapter, how heartening to hear those timeless words of Clare: 'And you have truly merited to be called a sister, spouse, and mother (2 Cor 11:2; Mt 12:50) of the Son of the Father of the Most High and of the glorious Virgin'.[33]

Having prayerfully explored some of the scriptural background presented in *Vita Consecrata*, in the context of Franciscan Religious Life and the call to be spouse, mother and sister, I would like, in the next chapter, to focus on those Scripture texts which give the context for identifying the different models of Religious Life: monastic, apostolic, mendicant/evangelical. We will explore the implications for leadership, prayer, ministry and community, the consequences of which will naturally lead to a deeper understanding of religious identity as it is lived by the various groups of consecrated men and women in the Church today.

Reflection

Bearing in mind the three objectives of the Year of Consecrated Life, where do you stand in relation to each one?

- Gratefully remembering the past
- Living the present with passion
- Embracing the future with hope

Notes

1   A. Flannery, OP, *Vatican Council II More Post Conciliar Documents*, vol, 2, 1982, *Lumen Gentium*, 43.
2   Pope John Paul II, *Vita Consecrata*, 14.

3 A. Flannery, OP, *Vatican Council II More Post Conciliar Documents*, vol. 2, *Evangelica Testificatio*, 29.
4 Pope John Paul II, *Vita Consecrata*, 1.
5 A. Grun, *Jesus, The Image of Humanity, Luke's Account*. New York, London: Continuum, 2003, p. 68.
6 Pope John Paul II, *Vita Consecrata*, 15.
7 Ibid., 19.
8 Congregation for Institutes of Consecrated Life and Societies of Apostolic Life, *Starting Afresh from Christ*. London: CTS, 2002, 23.
9 G. Weigel, *Evangelical Catholicism Deep Reform in the 21ᵗ Century Church*. New York: Basic Books, 2013, p. 172.
10 Pope John Paul II, *Vita Consecrata*, 104.
11 Ibid.
12 Ibid., 28.
13 Ibid.
14 Ibid., 34.
15 Ibid.
16 P. Jordan, FSM, *An Affair of the Heart, A Biblical and Franciscan Journey*. Leominster: Gracewing, 2006, p. 101.
17 Ibid.
18 R.J. Armstrong, OFMCap., W.J.A. Hellmann, OFM.Conv., W.J. Short, OFM, *Francis of Assisi, The Saint, Early Documents*, vol. I. London, New York: New City Press, 1999, p. 49.
19 Saint Clare, 'First Letter to Agnes', in *Francis and Clare, The Complete Works*. New York: Paulist Press, 1982, p. 91.
20 M. Schlosser, 'Mother, Sister, Bride: The Spirituality of Saint Clare', in *Greyfriars Review*, 5/2, 1991, p. 244.
21 Ibid., p. 245.
22 Saint Clare, 'Fourth Letter to Agnes', in *Francis and Clare, The Complete Works*, p. 205.
23 M. Schlosser, 'Mother, Sister, Bride: The Spirituality of Saint Clare', p. 234.
24 Saint Clare, 'Third Letter to Agnes', in *Francis and Clare, The Complete Works*, p. 201.
25 J. F. Godet, 'Clare the Woman, as Seen in her Writings', in *Greyfriars Review*, 4/3, 1990, p. 18.
26 Saint Clare, 'Third Letter to Agnes', in *Francis and Clare, The Complete Works*, p. 200.
27 Saint Clare, 'The Testament of Saint Clare', in *Francis and Clare, The Complete Works*, p. 231.

28 Ibid., pp. 227–8.
29 Saint Clare, 'Third Letter to Agnes', in *Francis and Clare, The Complete Works*, p. 200.
30 Saint Clare, 'Second Letter to Agnes', in *Francis and Clare, The Complete Works*, p. 197.
31 Pontifical Work for Ecclesiastical Vocations, *In Verbo Tuo*, by the Congregation for Institutes of Consecrated Life and Societies of Apostolic Life. Vatican, 1997, 13.
32 M. Schlosser, 'Mother, Sister, Bride: The Spirituality of Saint Clare', p. 234.
33 Saint Clare, 'First Letter to Agnes', in *Francis and Clare, The Complete Works*, p. 193.

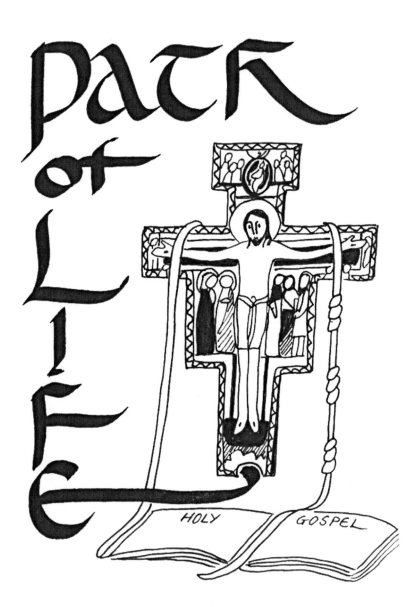

PATH of LIFE

HOLY   GOSPEL

Chapter Three

Discovering Who We Are

To be alive, the adaptation to the milieu does not consist in abandoning one's true identity, but rather in affirming it in its specific vitality.

(Evangelica Testificatio, 11)

The discovery of identity is a lifelong process for every person. Following one's personal vocation is the way to this discovery, and the graced revelation and response involved is the work of the Holy Spirit. In accepting the gift of a vocation to Religious Life, we become counter-cultural in that we do not follow the usual pattern that gives people identity and self-fulfilment: marriage, money, status symbols, career, fame and popularity. In this context, when speaking about the identity of Religious, Timothy Radcliffe gives two very good reasons for choosing to live the Gospel way of the counsels of poverty, chastity and obedience.

We do this so as to bring to light the true identity and vocation of every human being. First of all, we show that every human identity is gift. No self-created identity is ever adequate to who we are. Every little identity which we can hammer out in this society is just too small. And secondly, we show that human identity is not finally given now. It is the whole story of our lives, from beginning to end and beyond, that shows us who we are'.[1]

When a person responds to the gift of a Religious vocation within a particular Institute, the question 'Who am I?' also includes the question, 'Who are We?' and the latter is my main focus for this chapter, though the two identities cannot really be separated. While it is necessary to come to know and own the spiritual charism of the Institute to which I belong, it is also necessary to know how this institutional charism will help me become the person God has called me to be, also to be aware of the way in which I can make this institutional charism a reality in living out my own personal story.

In the previous chapter we pondered the privilege and challenge it is for Religious to make the features of Jesus constantly visible in the midst of the world, and it requires an understanding of the relationship that exists between personal identity and the spiritual identity of the Religious family to which I belong. This is not an easy task for the individual or the Institute, but we have been called to a 'creative fidelity' in living our various charisms. This requires humility, openness and a willingness to change in such a way that we are neither stuck in the past nor at the mercy of every whim in the present. Personal and Congregational responsibility is a delicate balance that recognises the uniqueness and gift of each one called to a certain Religious family, as well as the gift of the original charism, which in every age is called to make the face of God present in a particular way. We need to adapt and update the charism in a way

that recognises the uniqueness of every person called,
and also meets the needs of contemporary society. For
some this may appear to be fearful or threatening, but in
actual fact it is very exciting and bursting with new life
and potential for the individual and the group. As Fr
Paul Rivi, OFM Cap. writes:

> The values which characterise the charism of the family
> to which I belong reveal the name which God has given
> me, the features of my interior face which He created
> with the action of his Spirit. Without understanding this,
> the elements contained in the charism do not have the
> power to change my life.[2]

What a personal and Congregational challenge these
words present! But when a group is alive with the Spirit
and has a sense of the sacredness of every person's
unique and God-given call, then the face of Christ
becomes visible and the Gospel becomes the Good News
it is meant to be. The charism has the power to change
my life if I choose the life it offers as gift. 'Identity is a
gift, and the story of my life is made up of all those
choices to accept or refuse that gift'.[3] Choosing a particular Institute of Consecrated Life is both a privilege and a
responsibility, therefore, it is essential to really understand the Institute's charism from both an historical and
contemporary viewpoint. With this in mind I will briefly
outline the different models of Religious Life so that
each spiritual family will be able to recognise its roots
and the challenges involved. The outline will be in broad
brushstrokes with particular emphasis on Franciscan
Evangelical Life, which is my own lived experience.

The personal charism involved in founding an Institute of Consecrated Life is a grace given by God to founders and foundresses for the sake of fostering holiness in the Church, and responding, through their mission, to the challenges of the times. This is a free gift of the Holy Spirit, a special grace by which the Spirit makes a person or a group fit and ready for a specific service in renewing and upbuilding the Church, and thus making present the reign of God.

Before we look at the specifics of a lived charism in a given Institute, it is necessary to understand why Vatican Council II encouraged us to return to our founding charism in a way that penetrates every aspect of our Religious lives. I say this because, as Franciscans, we have discovered that many of us lived our Franciscan calling recognising and cherishing the charism of Francis, but modeling our everyday lives on the theology of the Dominican friar, St Thomas Aquinas, and the monastic ideals of St Benedict! It has been an exhilarating journey to discover that we actually have a different (not better – just different) way of being Religious. And the journey of discovery continues!

Many other apostolic Religious too adopted this model: Dominican theology, plus a monastic or semi-monastic lifestyle, while adding to these two the particular charism of their own Institute. This was especially true of women's communities, which had to follow the structures imposed on them by a Canon Law which did not offer the same freedom to women as it did to men.

Without going into a lengthy history of the development of Religious Life, which is outlined in *Vita*

Consecrata, basically we have different models which we can now term monastic, apostolic, and evangelical. Since Vatican II other forms of consecrated life have emerged and we will look at some of the new Congregations and Associations in a later chapter. For the moment I desire to delve a little deeper into the consequences of shaping a founding charism within contexts that blur the original vision and gift. This happened in the Franciscan Congregation to which I belong and also in the wider Franciscan Family. Other Orders and Congregations also have made the same discovery when responding to the clarion call of Vatican II to return to their sources. We all accepted the challenge with renewed vigour and enthusiasm, resulting in wonderful insights bringing new life and necessary change. In choosing to write from my own experience of Franciscan Religious Life since Vatican II, I hope other Religious can identify with some of the discoveries and apply them to their own lives.

When I entered Religious Life in the 1960s, I believed I was entering an 'active apostolic' Congregation as opposed to a 'contemplative enclosed' Order. Over the years, I have grown in my understanding of the various terms we use to identify different styles of Religious Life. One of the main discoveries has been the false notion of 'active' and 'contemplative'. The Congregation I entered seemed to me to have an apostolic/active thrust regarding ministry, but in many ways our lifestyle was somewhat monastic. At the same time, however, there was something unique within the lived experience of being sisters together and living the Gospel in the spirit of St Francis. This was experienced on a subconscious level rather than being articulated. I could not have put it into words then, but looking back I now recognize it as a way of being truly Franciscan.

I was not a Religious sister prior to Vatican II, but with hindsight I realize my Congregation, wisely I think, did not rush into change and adaptation. Consequently, many external practices, which were definitely pre-Vatican II, did not sit comfortably with me in those early days of Religious Life. But something within this group of people *did* 'fit', and I stayed. This meant I was caught up in those heady post-Vatican II days when doors were opening encouraging us to examine and explore who we were, not just as individuals but also as a group. Perhaps it was a bit easier for us because we were not even 100 years old at the time of Vatican II, so we were still in the process of discovering, understanding, developing and articulating our particular charism. For us, as Franciscans, we had a long journey ahead, and it continues with a freshness and newness that is always received as a gift of the Holy Spirit. *Vita Consecrata* reminds us:

> Communion in the Church is not uniformity, but a gift of the Spirit who is present in the variety of charisms and states of life. These will be all the more helpful to the Church and her mission the more their specific identity is respected.[4]

Different Models of Religious Life

Before delving more deeply into the Franciscan Movement and our continuing journey of discovery, I would like to outline briefly and simply something of the models of Religious Life that were prevalent at the time of Vatican II. Most people will be familiar with the terms 'active' and 'contemplative' Orders. The former was a blanket term for all Religious Institutes involved in active ministry, otherwise known as apostolates of various types – for example, education, nursing, social and missionary work. Contemplative was a blanket term used for all those who lived an enclosed monastic lifestyle. In addition there were semi-enclosed Institutes who lived a monastic lifestyle but were also involved in an apostolate, usually attached to the convent or monastery.

Most Religious today will recognize these broad categories, but change came when Religious were challenged to return to their roots and discover their original charism or gift. I think this is an on-going search because the charism is not something static but comes to life in the people who are called to a particular Institute. As Pope Francis recently stated, 'The charism is not a bottle of distilled water. It needs to be lived energetically as well as reinterpreted culturally'.[5] Over the years, charisms were blurred by a uniformity that emerged and, to a great extent cramped the original gift of the Spirit, due, as has already been said, by some of the strictures placed on women by Canon Law. Later in this chapter, readers will be invited to ponder the main areas of distinction that characterises monastic, apostolic and evangelical Religious Life. I speak mainly from the Franciscan experience with which I am most familiar.

Let us now look briefly at the biblical foundation for the different forms of Religious Life and the distinctive elements attached to them. Later in the chapter we will see how Church Documents have influenced the way in which Religious Life continues to be defined.

The Biblical Basis for Monastic Religious Life

The biblical foundation for monastic life is based on a verse from the Acts of the Apostles: 'The whole group of believers was united, heart and soul; no one claimed private ownership of any possessions, as everything they owned was held in common' (4:32). This text informed a lifestyle that was characterised by an apostolate of formal liturgical prayer, stability of place and withdrawal from the world. It highlighted the importance of liturgy and music, art and architecture, all of which pointed to heaven rather than earth. It emphasised a 'leaving the world' and entering a 'heavenly dimension'. Physical presence together in community and in the routine and regularity of life together, whether praying, eating, reading, working or recreating, was also very important. Some of these aspects can be recognised as forming not only monastic communities, but also many active apostolic Religious communities. *Vita Consecrata* sums up the place of monasticism in these words:

> In the heart of the Church and the world, monasteries have been and continue to be eloquent signs of communion, welcoming abodes for those seeking God and the things of the spirit, schools of faith and true places of study, dialogue and culture and of the earthly city itself, in expectation of the heavenly city.[6]

The Biblical Basis for Apostolic Religious Life

In the thirteenth century when Francis of Assisi became aware of his unique gift and calling from the Lord 'to

live according to the Gospel', apostolic life meant
something different from our understanding of this
lifestyle today. In Francis's day 'vita apostolica' was
associated with newer forms of Religious Life that
combined communal living with itinerant preaching.
The biblical basis was the missionary discourses in the
Gospels, either Matthew 10 or Luke 9. Though not identifying completely with these texts as a form of life, St
Francis was deeply influenced by them.

> He called the twelve together and gave them power and
> authority over all devils and to cure diseases, and He
> sent them out to proclaim the Kingdom of God and to
> heal. He said to them, 'Take nothing for the journey:
> neither staff, nor haversack, nor bread, nor money, and
> do not have a spare tunic. Whatever house you enter,
> stay there; and when you leave let your departure be
> from there. As for those who do not welcome you, when
> you leave their town shake the dust from your feet as
> evidence against them.' So they set out and went from
> village to village proclaiming the good news and healing
> everywhere (Lk 9:1–6).

As pointed out by the Franciscan historian, Joseph
Chinnici, apostolic Religious Life has undergone significant changes and great transformation since the
thirteenth century. 'After the sixteenth century the term
came to be associated primarily with those Religious
involved in an active apostolate.'[7] In the same
document, Chinnici goes on to say that in the Church it
has become customary to see the major portion of
Religious Life as 'vita apostolica'. He sees this emphasis
in the *Code of Canon Law*, in *The Essential Elements of*

Religious Life and in U.I.S.G. Document *Apostolic Spirituality in View of the Kingdom* – all three of which we will examine later. For our present purposes, I merely wish to point to the primary characteristic defining apostolic Religious Life since the sixteenth century: active involvement in diverse apostolates. Such activity involved a certain amount of mobility, availability and flexibility in establishing the Kingdom of God and building up the Church in the world. This was and continues to be the spirit and purpose of apostolic Religious Life as *Vita Consecrata* recognises.

> This is a splendid and varied testimony, reflecting the multiplicity of gifts bestowed by God on founders and foundresses who, in openness to the working of the Holy Spirit, successfully interpreted the signs of the times and responded to new needs.[8]

The Biblical Basis for Franciscan Evangelical Life

Francis believed with all his heart that God, the Most High, revealed to him a form of living that was a unique Gospel gift. So, what is this Gospel gift and how is it different from the monastic and apostolic forms of Religious Life? In attempting to answer this question, it is important to remember the words of Francis: 'The Most High Himself revealed to me to live according to the form of the holy Gospel'.[9] This way of life for Francis, and ultimately for the whole Franciscan Movement, was not monastic life, based on the first community as depicted in the Acts of the Apostles, nor was it all apostolic life based on the missionary discourses in the Gospels of St Matthew and St Luke. It was something new.

The beginning of the Rule of Life for the four Families that make up the Franciscan Order as a whole – Friars Minor, Poor Clares, Third Order Regular and Secular Franciscans – state very simply that our form of life is: 'To observe the holy Gospel of Our Lord Jesus Christ'. From what we have said it is obvious that every form of Religious Life is rooted in the Word of God. And as pointed out by the Franciscan scholar, Fr Regis Armstrong, 'The Monastic Religious Life envisions entrance into a world shaped and molded by the Word'.[10] He also concludes that 'Apostolic Religious Life burns with the desire to proclaim the Word to all peoples'.[11] So where does Franciscan Evangelical Life focus its desire and attention? According to Armstrong, like the monastic and apostolic forms of Religious Life, the Franciscan way is also a response to God's Word. However, 'What makes the Franciscan approach so unique is its focus not on structure or activity, place or time, occupation or status, but simply on the human heart where the Word dwells'.[12] Intimacy with the Word, becoming a dwelling place for the Word, has far-reaching consequences regarding how we see God, ourselves, each other, and our world. It is as Armstrong says, 'a life caught up in relationships'.[13] It is this focus on the heart where the Word dwells that captures for me the essence of living Franciscan Evangelical Religious Life, affecting as it does every aspect of relational living. Later in this chapter I will point to the way in which such a Gospel response affects prayer, ministry, leadership, fraternity – all aspects of

Religious Life – unified and integrated in the Word dwelling within the heart.

While Francis did not identify with either the monastic or the apostolic model, he did incorporate aspects of both into his way of life. He knew that for him the emphasis was to live as Christ lived *with* his disciples. In other words, it was not one aspect of the Gospel but a radical living of the whole Gospel, following in the footprints of Jesus. 'He focused his life neither on prayer, nor on ministry, but on the person, the person of Jesus Christ'.[14] It follows that the dignity of the human person made in his image, and in relationship with others, will be key in understanding a Franciscan vocation. And we live our consecrated lives so as to bring to light the true identity and vocation of every human being.

To do this, Franciscan Evangelical Religious Life focuses on the Incarnation, the mystery of God's self revelation in Jesus Christ and its meaning and conse-quences for every human person and the whole of creation. What it means to be human and to be in rela-tionship lies at the heart of our on-going challenge to articulate our Franciscan Evangelical heritage.

> The Evangelical Religious Life means witness – witness as a Roman Catholic to the good Gospel of Our Lord Jesus Christ. It means taking seriously and publicly naming the fact that God, who encompasses all things, is the personal heart of the Evangelical Life and the goal of our desires. It means talking about this search for God, a community of Three in One, Whose Word became flesh in the womb of a woman, and giving it a social language which communi-cates to people who our God is and who we are.[15]

Stages of Growth and Development

As a Movement and worldwide family, Franciscans have recognised at least three major stages of revitalization in our understanding of who we are.[16] Perhaps our stages of growth and development will also sound a familiar note for Religious in other spiritual families. First of all, following on from Vatican II, there was serious study of the Documents of the Council, especially *Lumen Gentium* 6 and *Perfectae Caritatis*. For example, we are reminded in *Lumen Gentium* that the hierarchy 'uses its supervisory and protective authority too to ensure that Religious Institutes established all over the world for building up the Body of Christ may develop and flourish in accordance with the spirit of their founders'.[17] The same message is proclaimed in *Perfectae Caritatis*:

> It is for the good of the Church that institutes have their own proper characters and functions. Therefore the spirit and aims of each founder should be faithfully accepted and retained, as indeed should each institute's sound traditions, for all of these constitute the patrimony of an institute.[18]

With great enthusiasm and excitement Religious set about discovering or rediscovering their original charism and renewing their spiritual families in the light of this discovery. For the Franciscan Family, the first stage of renewal was an institutional one, lasting for a lengthy period from the end of the Vatican Council in 1965 until 1982. During this period we were involved in the rewriting of new Franciscan Rules and revised Constitutions, which were completed and approved by the Church. Also during that period we had the first critical translation of the writings of Francis and Clare, called *The Omnibus of Sources*. I treasured mine when my sisters presented me with the *Omnibus* as a gift – a source for my ministry in formation. But this was only the beginning!

In 1982, with the publication of the new *Third Order Regular Franciscan Rule* (TOR), we delighted in the shared charism of Third Order Regular Franciscans, men and women like us throughout the world. I was amazed to discover that there were over 419 TOR Franciscan Congregations, all of whom were consulted in writing our revised TOR Rule, which was approved by Pope John Paul II in 1982. 'Never before in the Order's history have the members exercised such collective responsibility and global communication'.[19] I feel very privileged and I am deeply grateful to have engaged in that graced and challenging process. Also, having studied and compared in depth previous TOR Rules, I knew we had a precious and inspirational Form of Life to cherish and pass on to future generations.

This was an amazing time for us as TOR Franciscans. We embraced our newly approved Rule with great enthusiasm and, as we participated in workshops especially designed to unpack the spiritual riches of our Franciscan heritage, we felt we had received our birthright. As a Congregation, we were very fortunate in receiving inspirational and insightful talks and reflections from two of the seven people who formed the original Franciscan International Commission, the

Working Group for the re-writing of the TOR Rule: Margaret Carney, OSF, and Thaddeus Horgan, SA. Margaret has been described as 'both the message and the messenger of a vibrant rediscovery of TOR life and rule'.[20]

Grounded in biblical spirituality, with special emphasis on the four fundamental Gospel values of conversion of heart, contemplation, minority (humility) and poverty, together with the writings of St Francis, our Rule was (and continues to be) spirit and life to us. We cherished and shared its contents, renewing ourselves ever more deeply as individuals and communities.

In addition to the four fundamental values mentioned above, each of the 400-plus TOR Franciscan Congregations also embarked on discovering the distinctive charism of their individual Congregation. Before writing a small booklet on our Congregational charism as Franciscan Minoress Sisters, I remember writing to every Sister in our Congregation. I was deeply moved by their responses as I collated the material for a General Chapter presentation for our Congregation. What was written and shared came from our hearts and lived experience. That was 1982–1983. These were very exciting times but we could not have envisaged what lay ahead.

From 1983 until 1996 we delved more deeply into identifying our distinctive charism as Franciscans. As one Franciscan scholar said, 'Contemporary Franciscan Life has become shapeless because our theology has become eclectic, the result of a fragmented evangelical synthesis of theology and lived experience'.[21] This came to the fore in the early 1990s but it had its beginnings in the 1980s with the publication of three documents that affected the fabric and identity, even the structure of our lives. These documents had a profound affect on our Franciscan search for a distinct Franciscan identity: the *New Code of Canon Law*, the *Essential Elements of Religious Life* and the U.I.S.G. document *Apostolic Spirituality*. Later in the Chapter we will look at each of these briefly in relation to our present topic. The challenge to articulate our distinctive charism came in response to these publications, which made no mention of many core values of our Franciscan Tradition. Consequently, our Franciscan family as a whole began to articulate a new institutional option called Franciscan Evangelical Life. This formulation set us apart from both the monastic life and the apostolic life as our distinctive way of being in the world.

Prior to the publication of the above three documents, each of the spiritual families that make up the worldwide Franciscan Movement had laboured to identify their own Congregational charism. As most readers will know, there are four main branches within the worldwide family of St Francis: the First Order of Friars Minor including the Conventuals and the Capuchins, the Second Order of Poor Clares, the Third Order Regular and the Order of Secular Franciscans. From research into the distinctive charism of each individual branch, a further question emerged: what is our distinctive charism as Franciscans irrespective of whether we belong to the First, Second or Third Orders?

In trying to answer this question I am indebted to two people in particular: Fr Regis Armstrong, OFMCap., laid a solid foundation with his writings on the Word of God and the place of the heart in understanding our tradition. And Sr Kathleen Moffatt, OSF, who gave us a workshop as we prepared for our General Chapter in 2009, which was intended to be a celebration of Franciscan Evangelical Life. The materials shared by Sr Kathleen which were based on the work of Franciscan scholars, particularly Fr Joseph Chinnici, OFM, Jean-Francois Godet and the late Fr Thaddeus Horgan, TOR, have been used to articulate our Franciscan identity. We acknowledge the tremendous contribution of Sr Kathleen in making these materials accessible to us. We are now in a position not only to ask the fundamental questions, but also, thanks to the scholars, we have the beginnings of possible answers.

As a Congregation, we continue to unpack the riches of the insights we have received in embracing our Franciscan heritage in new ways. In an effort to define our life as Franciscan Sisters Minoress, we can say that we desire to give birth to Christ in our hearts and in the world, so that those we meet on the journey of life may be touched by his living presence in our midst. 'Evangelical life is attentiveness to the human person as the revelation of God; thus, Incarnation defines the Life'.[22] The Word became flesh and dwelt among us and continues to dwell within us. This is the heart of the matter.

In an effort to articulate our self-understanding, and the consequences of recognising our unique gift in the Church and the world, a Schema was developed by the late Fr Thaddeus Horgan, SA, and Sister Jeanine Moro-zowich, CSSF. This Schema presented a brief overview of Monastic, Apostolic and Evangelical Religious Life.

Our background for studying the Schema below is our primary call to live the Gospel, following in the footprints of Jesus, Son of God and Brother to all. In so doing the heart is central because it is the dwelling place of the Word of God. It is in the heart that we are attentive, receptive and responsive to the Word. The Word became flesh and dwelt among us. In and through and with Christ our Brother, we share in the extravagant love of a God who calls us into the fullness of life and love within the Trinity, with each other, and in fraternal relationship with the whole of creation. As Armstrong says:

> The interiorisation and incarnation of the word of God: that is, in essence, the life that Francis envisions ... The Evangelical life then, is quite simple; one might say simplicity is its hallmark. It consists in cultivating the heart so that it becomes the perfect soil in which God's seed can thrive and bear fruit'.[23]

	Monastic	Apostolic	Evangelical
FOCUS	Teach members the practice of the Christian life especially through prayer in common.	Founded primarily for mission and ministry.	To live as Christ did as this is portrayed in the Gospels, specifically by total and continuous conversion of heart and by becoming a dwelling place for the Lord.

	Monastic	Apostolic	Evangelical
PRAYER	Personally contemplative, communally liturgical and the primary characteristic of lifestyle.	Personally contem plative, on a regular basis active prayerful presence in the midst of the Church. Office simple; community observances determined by the ministry.	Personally contemplative; communally liturgical and shared; centred on Scripture especially the Gospels.
MINISTRY	Prayer: the Lectio Divina and the Church's liturgy.	Establishment and strengthening the life of the Church in service and mission.	The manifestation of the fruits befitting conver sion of the heart (Mt 25:34ff) especially peacemaking.
COMMUNITY	Communal presence essential to meals, prayer, recreating and work.	Based on shared faith vision and common apostolic goal(s).	Fraternity – *all* are brothers and sisters gathered by the Spirit to live conscious that Christ is Brother to all; emphasis on relationship.
LEADERSHIP	Abbot/Abbess: teacher of spiritual life, administrator of abbey. Some decision-making hierarchic, others communal.	Animator who fosters life and ministry and helps members spiritually in view of apostolic goal(s), decision-making based on goals.	Servant of the fraternity, its link-person who preserves and fosters the fraternal relation ship by calling all to fulfil all that they have promised the Lord (The Rules).

	Monastic	Apostolic	Evangelical
MODEL	Acts of the Apostles – sharing all things in common.	Primitive apostolic community in its efforts at establishing the Church.	Life of disciples with Jesus who learned the values of solitude, relationship and service-ministry from the example of Christ's own life.
OTHER CHARACTERISTICS	Common life, manual labour, regularity and stability (set apart from the world in order to be part of it). This is the lifestyle of Poor Clares and Carmelites nuns but the *model* is not the Acts of the Apostles.	Mobility, availability, flexibility for the sake of effective active ministry.	Active contemplative prayerful lifestyle marked by simplicity, service and fraternal relationship. These characteristics belong to the whole Franciscan Movement and also to Carmelites.

Brother Ed Coughlin, OFM, also provided a Schema detailing aspects of our inner tensions common to Monastic, Apostolic and Franciscan Evangelical Religious Life. See below. I would add a comment about cloistered Religious in the evangelical/mendicant tradition. Although they do not 'go out on mission' their lives are their witness and their preaching, as they become for the world an example and mirror of Gospel living.

FORMS	LIFESTYLES	SPIRITUALITY
Monastic – emphasis is on place, order, routine, regularity, discipline of the spiritual life. – purpose is to grow in personal holiness in the context of common life and prayer. – structure (place) centred around the liturgical life and the promotion of a life in solitude and recollection "the cloister". (Benedictines/Cistercians/Canons Regular)	**Community** – emphasis is on the observance of the horarium and the performance of designated functions. – leaders are to direct the life and ministry of the members (top-down). – individuals have delegated responsibility to fill needed roles and functions. – everyone knows 'their place' and their role.	**Personal** – Search for God through a personal relationship pursued primarily in prayer/contemplation. – emphasis on: – private, personal relationship with God. – the vertical dimension (to God above). – ministry flows from private prayer. – goal is to become a man/woman of of prayer.
Evangelical/Mendicant – emphasis is on 'following in the footprints of Christ' in 'the company of my brothers and sisters'. – purpose is the shared desire 'to live the Gospel as lesser brothers/sisters' – be an evangelising fraternity. – structure provides a context for brothers/sisters who can share prayer, values, fraternal life, and from which they go out on mission. 'on the way, 'the world is our cloister'. (Franciscans/Dominicans/Carmelites)	**Fraternity** – emphasis is on: – interdependence – mutuality – reciprocity – leadership's function is to facilitate the interaction and dialogue that leads to decisions which aim at achieving shared mission (participative style). – individuals are committed to living and working together to realise a shared mission. – collaborators in mission.	**Relational** Searching for God in prayer, in the bonds of fraternal relationships, as well as in the loving service of one's neighbour. – emphasis on – personal prayer – interpersonal relationships – shared faith experience – both the horizontal and the vertical. – ministry flows from personal prayer and fraternal life (common prayer, shared faith, supportive personal relationships). – goal is contemplation and action.

Apostolic	Association of Vowed Members	Ministerial
– emphasis on the pastoral needs of the Church in the world. – purpose is to render service to those in need in the name of the Church. – structure is determined by the ministerial situation. 'where we are most needed'. (Jesuits/Christian Brothers)	– emphasis is on each individual sharing his/her talents and gifts in the service of the Church/world. – leadership's function is to support and encourage individual development as well as responsiveness to emerging needs (bottom-up). – independence with a measure of connectedness. – co-workers/co-operators.	Searching for God in the world, in the the loving service of those who are in need. – emphasis on – relationship of service to the other. – the horizontal dimension (to God in the other/world). – ministry is a way of praying (less time devoted to either private or communal prayer). – goal is to become a contemplative in action.

As a Congregation, our search continues as we try to live the Gospel in the spirit of St Francis, with the 'creative fidelity' asked of us by the Church. We are aware of the courage needed to move out of our comfort zones and make the Good News of the Gospel a reality, with the newness that inflamed the heart of Francis of Assisi.

Our Foundress, Mother Francis Murphy, was among the number of those valiant women who struggled to keep alive and present a new face of Franciscan evangelical life. It is beyond the scope of this book to present the history of the development of Third Order Regular Congregations but others have admirably undertaken and completed this task.[24] In every age God raises up men and women to find new ways of reaching people's hearts in answering contemporary needs.

To be spiritually faithful to Francis it is not enough to
immerse ourselves in historical Franciscanism, like
living in a hothouse in which we can isolate ourselves
from our context; we should instead try to interpret the
evangelical path of Francis, with its unique and particular characteristics, to find new ways of expressing it, that
are comprehensible, eloquent and prophetic for the
people of our time.[25]

Our emphasis on being brothers and sisters is central to
understanding our Franciscan identity. We were not
founded for any particular apostolic work. It is our call
to be brother, to be sister, which affects the diversity of
ministries and gifts we find within our Franciscan
family. For us, as for our spiritual father, St Francis, the
world is our cloister, a place sanctified by the Incarnate
Lord when he lived and walked on our earth.

Rooted in Incarnational spirituality, the two schemas
presented in chart form outline distinguishing characteristics relating to the three forms of Religious Life.
Such studies have helped us in our search to retrieve and
name our distinctive charism and mission in the Church
and the world. And while there are many wonderful and
inspiring articles on this topic, the Schemas show at a
glance the diversity and uniqueness of the different spiritualities which have enriched, and continue to enrich
the Church and the world today.

For Francis, the consequences of being in loving relationship with the Trinitarian God immersed him in a
world of fraternal intimacy with the whole of created
reality. Welcoming the New Year 2014, Pope Francis
prayed that the 'Gospel of fraternity' might 'speak to

every conscience and knock down the walls that hinder enemies from recognising each other as brothers and sisters'.[26] Such an inclusive vision lies at the heart of living according to the Holy Gospel by following in the footprints of Jesus Christ in the spirit of St Francis of Assisi. Such close following of Christ leads to the experience of fraternity and the call to witness to it in a very real way wherever we are and whatever we are doing. The charism of fraternity is a fundamental and unifying characteristic among the diverse groups of friars, Poor Clare nuns, Third Order Regular brothers and sisters and secular Franciscans within the large family of St. Francis. 'The person, as the fundamental category in Franciscan experience, can be any place or do anything within the Gospel and still be a Franciscan'.[27] Because Jesus, the Son of God is our brother, the Franciscan Order(s) exist for the purpose of brotherhood/sisterhood, which defines the character and spirit of its presence and ministry in the world. It is our recognised tool of evangelisation.

> 'After the Lord gave me brothers' ... was a clear watershed in the life of Francis. From that time on, he always saw the call to be brother as his primary response to the holy Gospel. In the end, he felt a loving relationship with everyone and everything ... Through grace, Francis arrived at the point where there was no violence or division within him, nothing to divide him from his neighbor or creation. This quality of brotherhood encountered in Francis and his early fraternity opened human hearts to the message of the holy Gospel. Brotherhood was his chosen tool of evangelization.[28]

Truly, the world is our cloister, therefore, neither withdrawal from the world nor action within it, are adequate
categories for our way of life, though both have a place.
The genius of Francis is that he melded elements from
both the monastic and apostolic traditions of his time,
yet did not identify wholly with either. Francis
embraced the communal tradition of the monastic life
without being bound by structures and regularity of
time and place. He also embraced the itinerant nature of
the apostolic life of his time, but this was always limited
by the fraternal commitment to, and presence with, his
brothers. Such a synthesis is the genius of Francis, and
this is the reason why he could not make an either/or
choice from the Religious Life forms that were available
to him. Rather, his was a both/and position, located on
the level of the person (rather than a place or a ministry),
and this understanding and vision led to a unique gift of
Religious Life within the Church. For varied historical
reasons the vision was lost to some extent through the
centuries, but periods of renewal and the vision of individuals have always kept it alive, hence the presence
and vitality of Franciscan life in the world today. With
renewed enthusiasm, we continue the struggle to name
our gift within the Church and to witness to it in fidelity
to the charism we have received. One Franciscan scholar
puts it this way:

> To give an account of the hope that is within us. That is
> our challenge ... We have hope within us, within our
> intellectual and spiritual tradition. We have a hopeful
> word to speak to concerns present in today's Church and
> to crises affecting our society ... We are holding inside us
> a word that can speak to these questions.[29]

This synthesis is now being lived out in our own Congregation. We are involved in all kinds of active ministries, but we also have a House of Franciscan Solitude based on St Francis's Rule for Hermitages. Our journey of discovery has led us to a deeper understanding and embrace of the following of Christ in a way that integrates contemplation and action. 'Here is a vision of life that transcends the duality of active vs. contemplative, of practical vs. theoretical, of apostolic vs. cloistered'.[30] These words from a Religious who is not a Franciscan, is music to our ears. She understands that our way of living Religious Life is a viable life-form based on intimate union with, and imitation of, the Person of Jesus as revealed in the Gospels, and she summarises our challenge in a threefold manner:

• As a viable form of Religious Life
• As a mode of theological reflection
• As a way of seeing the world and all persons in it[31]

And from her understanding and lived experience as a sister in an apostolic Congregation, Mary Beth Ingham offers the following example of the distinction between apostolic and evangelical Religious Life. I think it is worth quoting in full because of its interest to all Religious.

> For an apostolic institute such as mine, community life follows from the apostolate. In other words, how we live and where we live depends upon our apostolic ministry. For an evangelical institute, by contrast, how one lives and where one lives are primary, not secondary. Their form of life is their witness. And what's more, their

apostolic work derives from their community life. At a deeper spiritual level, we might say that their life is their apostolic work, since the praxis of the Franciscan family is to bear witness to their life with one another and in the Lord.[32]

We are at this moment in history because we have responded to the call of the Church to return to our original charism. In attempting to do this, we have had to dialogue with existing insights, reflections and documents, especially the *New Code of Canon Law*, the *Essential Elements of Religious Life* and the U.I.S.G. document *Apostolic Spirituality*. Let us look briefly at these documents and the ways in which they have helped us to clarify the gift we have been given.

Code of Canon Law

The Code of Canon Law published in 1983 mentions Monastic and Apostolic Religious Life but makes no mention of Evangelical Religious Life. Because of their relevance to our present reflections, it is worth quoting the following Canons in full.

Institutes which are wholly directed to contemplation always have an outstanding part in the mystical Body of Christ. They offer to God an exceptional sacrifice of praise. They embellish the people of God with very rich fruits of holiness, move them by their example, and give them increase by a hidden apostolic fruitfulness. Because of this, no matter how urgent the needs of the active apostolate, the members of these institutes cannot be called upon to assist in the various pastoral ministries.

Apostolic action is of the very nature of institutes dedicated to apostolic works. The whole life of the members is, therefore, to be imbued with an apostolic spirit, and the whole of their apostolic action is to be animated by a religious spirit.

Apostolic action is always to proceed from intimate union with God, and is to confirm and foster this union. Apostolic action exercised in the name of the Church and by its command is to be performed in communion with the Church. [33]

While having full Church approval for our way of life, Franciscans and other mendicants do not fall within either of these clear-cut canonical categories. While a third category of Religious Life is not mentioned in the Code at present, we realise that within the Franciscan Family worldwide, we identify in some ways with all four categories: contemplative, monastic, apostolic and secular institutes, yet no single category seemed to 'fit' our family.[34] As we continue to strive for self-understanding and to name our unique expression of Religious Life, we are heartened to find many references in the *Code* that stress the importance of being faithful to the original charism. The following is one such example.'The intention of the founders and their determination concerning the nature, purpose, spirit and character of the Institute are to be observed faithfully by all'.[35] This gives a wonderful freedom to explore, discover, clarify and articulate our unique identity. Mother Church is asking us to be faithful to our inheritance: we are called to live according to the Gospel of Our Lord Jesus Christ. Readers may well say that living the Gospel is the call of every Christian. This is true, but for Franciscans there is a particular significance, which highlights the originality of the Franciscan charism.

We have already referred to the words St Francis wrote in his *Testament,* when he recalled a very important moment in his faith journey, one that has consequences for his followers until the end of time. It bears repeating because of its significance: 'The Most High Himself revealed to me that I should live according to the form of the Holy Gospel'.[36] Francis knew what he wanted: life according to the Gospel (*vita evangeli*), not monastic life (*vita monastica*), and not apostolic life (*vita apostolica*). This was a very decisive moment in the life of Francis, and it continues to shape the Franciscan family today. When Church authorities and even some of his own brothers wanted him to adopt an already existing way of Religious Life, Francis rejected other choices that were available to him at that time, saying, 'I do not want you to mention to me any Rule, whether of St Augustine, or of St Bernard or of St Benedict. The Lord told me what he wanted'.[37] Speaking of this conviction in the heart of Francis, one Franciscan scholar says, 'Given the apostolic movements of his day, there was something which he considered to be unique about the Lord's gift to him'.[38] In this revelation to Francis lies our search for understanding what this means for us today in the twenty-first century. It leads us straight back to the nature, purpose and spirit of why we exist as a particular group within the Church, a point we will continue to develop in this chapter, but first I would like to mention briefly the way in which we express the originality of the Franciscan charism as Third Order Regular Franciscan Minoress Sisters.

Franciscan Minoress Charism

Like many Congregations founded in the nineteenth and twentieth centuries, our Congregation came to birth in a time of crisis, emerging from a people in crisis – the world's poor little ones. Our Foundress, Sister Francis Murphy, was already a Religious Sister with the Poor Servants of the Mother of God, but she experienced a spiritual imperative not unlike that of Mother Teresa of Calcutta. She was impelled by the insistent voice of the Holy Spirit to leave familiar religious paths to answer a new obedience.[39] This was a call to respond to the crisis of the poor and destitute in the spirit of St Francis of Assisi, her chosen patron. As our Constitutions so aptly state: 'In choosing a rule which resonated with her own inner spirit, Mother Francis chose to follow the Rule of the Third Order Regular of St Francis'.[40] Like St Francis who tells us that from the very beginning of his conversion, the Lord Himself led him among lepers (the poor and marginalised of his day) and Francis had mercy on them, so too our Foundress identified with the poor and the marginalised in her day. Such attentiveness to the dignity of the human person as the revelation of God is one of the hallmarks of evangelical life. As a Congregation, it has been remarked that we are 'incredibly itinerant' in the way we change and adapt to the changing needs of our brothers and sisters, especially those most in need. It has been and continues to be an essential part of our history to move from place to place and take on new apostolates as needs arise. For some young women, this diversity and adaptability has drawn them to our particular Religious family.

Wherever we are and whatever the service, what remains constant for us is the call to be sisters and to show mercy. In a personal letter written from her mission station in Ethiopia, this is how our Sister Annunciata describes her experience in famine-stricken, war-torn Ethiopia.

> Mary and Francis – they were always at ease with the poor. They moved easily within their world. So, like Christ, like Mary, like Francis, we try to believe where faith is dark; where hope is painful; where love is crucified. The poorest of the poor here in Ethiopia ... they are such a lovely courteous people, I feel a great privilege to be among them.

This resonates with words written in our FSM Constitutions describing our charism which sums up our call to live as Minoress Sisters.

> Gifted by the Holy Spirit through St Francis and our Foundress, Mother Francis, we are trustees of our Congregation's charism. We praise and thank God for the precious gift of minority which enables us to live as Minoresses, 'little ones'. In joyful, childlike trust and humility we embrace a life of poverty and simplicity, entering into the self-emptying of Christ, who took on the form of a servant.[41]

Ours is a call to childlikeness and servanthood. The former expresses our very personal and intimate relationship with the Trinity, a living experience of what it means to be a beloved child of God. The latter expresses our very real relationship with one another, with our brothers and sisters, and with all creation.

Essential Elements in Church Teaching on Religious Life

A second document, *Essential Elements*,[42] issued by the Vatican in 1983, was instrumental in furthering the search for our originality and identity. Its contents applied to Institutes dedicated to works of the apostolate. It was the thrust of this document that made the Franciscan family feel, once again, that we had a unique gift that could not be expressed adequately within the categories of the monastic life or the apostolic life. Certainly there are aspects of both ways of life that also form part of the Franciscan vocation, but the emphasis is elsewhere and it is this that distinguishes our unique gift of the Holy Spirit.

According to the document, *Essential Elements*, Apostolic Religious Life is primarily concerned with living life modelled on the life of the Apostles in the early Church. When Jesus returned to the Father, he entrusted his mission to the Apostles. It was their mission and task to proclaim the resurrection of Christ and establish his Kingdom on earth by founding new Christian communities and establishing the Church to the ends of the earth. This was and continues to be an essential Gospel mission and task.

It is obvious from reading the Acts of the Apostles that there is a commissioning and a task to be done. For Apostolic Religious who embrace this way of life, there will be a focus on specific apostolates through which they will mediate a particular view of God and the world. Through his apostles, Jesus must tell people of the goodness of God in a world that needs redemption, through good works. The Kingdom will be realised in the various works of mercy and particularly through justice leading to peace. This is the proclamation and task of Apostolic Religious as they establish and organise themselves in the world.

If the model for Apostolic Religious Life is based on the model of the life of the Apostles after the Ascension of Christ, the Evangelical model is based on the model of Jesus *with* the disciples. This is why St Francis insisted on 'life according to the Holy Gospel'. The Gospels are the foundation for Franciscan Evangelical Life. It is a life of intimacy *with* Jesus. In this way of life, we are constantly focused on Jesus. It was the genius of Francis to live life by doing what Jesus did in his earthly life. Later generations of Franciscans tried to encapsulate this Gospel vision by emphasising conformity to Christ with special focus on asceticism and perfection. 'They in effect froze a dynamic motif like the "following of Christ" – which originally meant doing all that Christ did on earth, ... into an ascetical "conformity" to Christ'.[43] It will always be a challenge to return to the original charism. Exaggerations in one direction and aberrations in interpretation may cloud or even freeze the vision temporarily, but the Holy Spirit has ways and means of bringing us back to the original gift.

In Franciscan Evangelical Life, there is no distinction between action and contemplation in the sense that these distinctions define a way of life or periods in a particular way of life. Our life has been described as 'an integrated life of contemplative action'.[44] It is not my intention to focus on the many ways in which active and contemplative have been understood throughout the centuries, yet as one Franciscan scholar points out: 'We do need working definitions of the terms we are discussing'.[45] Therefore, when my Congregation was discerning the possibility of establishing a Franciscan House of Prayer and Solitude, we invited two Franciscan scholars to share their expertise and lived experience with us. First we asked Fr Michael Higgins, TOR, to lead us in a retreat to help us to understand these terms active and contemplative more deeply, especially as St Francis understood and lived them. We then invited Fr Andre Cirino, OFM, to lead us in a Solitude Retreat based on St Francis's Rule for Hermitages. Both experiences clarified and enriched our research and discernment. To both of them we are tremendously grateful.

Michael Higgins defines 'active' as our way of 'being in' the world. This broad definition relates to every aspect of our lives and not just to our restricted active ministry as understood in apostolic communities. 'The motif "apostolic life" is clearly insufficient to explain Francis'.[46] The all-inclusive definition of 'active' as 'a way of being' sits much more comfortably with Franciscans. It means that we do not overemphasise the apostolic life or compartmentalise it; rather we integrate the active and the contemplative as one way of life so that we can truly say Franciscan Evangelical Life is *both/and* rather than *either/or*. There is no definite apostolate, no specific task, and yet ours is a call to be in the world with a readiness to embrace all kinds of service that promotes the Gospel. Like our father, Francis, we feel called to be among our brothers and sisters, sharing in the enjoyment of God and making this experience available to others. Perhaps it is easier to see how this call is expressed in the lives of the friars and sisters who are engaged in active ministry. But it is no less true of our Poor Clare Sisters, and in her Testament Clare states quite emphatically:

> The Lord Himself not only has set us as an example and mirror for others, but also for our own sisters whom the Lord has called to our way of life, so that they in turn will be an example and mirror to those living in the world.[47]

In one sense it is very difficult to give a precise definition of Franciscan Evangelical Life other than that of life *with* Jesus and following in his footprints. Just as Jesus revealed the goodness of God and the joy of being in contemplative relationship with his Father and with all creation as our brothers and sisters, this is our call too. Like Jesus, it means embracing a loving servant role as we minister to one another, upholding and creating peace in the variety of ways that present themselves. Our call to brotherhood/sisterhood is the consequence of being a dwelling place for the Word of God and shaping our hearts accordingly.

The Synod of Bishops on Consecrated Life in the Church, 1994

In the light of the 1994 Synod on Consecrated Life in the Church, the Franciscan Federation of the Third Order Regular responded to the *Lineamenta*, outlining once again the uniqueness of Franciscan Evangelical Religious Life, stating that 'The Franciscan charism is always and everywhere unbounded', reminding the

Synod that the world is our cloister. Part of our response included the following description of our way of life.

> In our Evangelical Life we have no dichotomies. We are not sometimes contemplative and sometimes active; now in community and then in mission. We stand with the poor while not ignoring the needs of others. This life has been and continues to be pondered and inculturated. In each century Franciscans have tried to read the signs of the times and responded to them appropriately. However, some essentials remain constant.[48]

We hope that the reflection in this chapter and indeed throughout this book, will voice our 'essentials that remain constant'. In so doing, the call to retrieve and name the beliefs at the core of our identity becomes a central focus: the goodness and humility of God, the primacy of Christ, the dignity of the human person and of creation. Our responses to these core beliefs manifest themselves in relationships of brotherhood and sisterhood with everyone and everything. We know that fraternal life is common to all institutes of Consecrated Life but it is the *purpose* of fraternity that distinguishes our Franciscan family from other Institutes in the Church. Because of our emphasis on the Word dwelling in our hearts and the consequences of this indwelling, we realise that we exist for the purpose of brotherhood and sisterhood in the Church and the world. It is this that defines our presence within the diverse ministries in which we are involved. This is our identity and unique gift in and for the Church and the world. In other words, the Incarnation – the mystery of God becoming human in Christ – challenges us to reveal what it means to be human by following in his footprints. In so doing, we will 'bring to light the true identity and vocation of every human being'.[49]

This experience of the Vita Evangelica demands further exploration. It should not be confused with the other charisms which exist within the Religious Life of the Church: the Vita Monastica and the Vita Apostolica. To confuse the three would be to deny our own history, the tradition which our founders Francis and Clare have given to us, and our call to witness in the Church and in the world. This call to live 'according to the form of the holy Gospel' is a unique gift.[50]

Like St Francis and St Clare, may we continue to be open to 'Divine inspiration', as we seek to live our Franciscan Evangelical charism with 'creative fidelity' today in the twenty– first century.

Reflection

Who/what has helped you to develop a sense of your unique identity and how has your chosen vocation in life contributed to this?

Notes

1 T. Radcliffe, 'The Identity of Religious Today', *Keynote Address to the U.S. Conference of Major Superiors of Men* (CMSM), August 8, 1996.
2 P. Rivi, OFMCap., *This is Me, A Journey through the Sources to Discover the Real Francis*. Italy: Edizioni Porziuncula, p. 17.
3 T. Radcliffe, 'The Identity of Religious Today', 1996.
4 *Vita Consecrata*, 4.
5 A. Sparado, SJ, 'Wake Up the World. Conversation with Pope Francis about Religious Life', in *La Civilta Cattolica*, 2014, pp. 6–7.

6 Ibid., p. 11.
7 J. P. Chinnici, OFM, 'Evangelical and Apostolic Tensions' in *Our Franciscan Charism Today*. New Jersey: Fame, 1987. Reprinted in *Franciscan Studies*, 55. New York: St Bonaventure University, 1998, p. 96.
8 *Vita Consecrata*, 9.
9 R. Armstrong, OFMCap., *et al*, 'The Testament in Francis of Assisi' in *The Saint*, vol. 1, p. 125.
10 R. Armstrong, OFMCap., 'If My Words Remain in You. Foundations of the Evangelical Life', in *Francis of Assisi, History, Hagiography and Hermeneutics in the Early Documents*, ed. by J. Hammond. London: New City Press, 2004, p. 75.
11 Ibid.
12 Ibid., p. 76.
13 Ibid.
14 J. P. Chinnici, 'Evangelical and Apostolic Tensions', p. 100.
15 Ibid,, p. 298.
16 K. Moffatt, *FSM General Chapter Workshop PPT Presentation on Evangelical Life*, 2009.
17 *Lumen Gentium*, 45.
18 *Perfectae Caritatis*, 2(b).
19 M. Carney, *The Rule and Life of the Brothers and Sisters of the Third Order Regular of St. Francis and Commentary*, 1983, p. 7.
20 I. Peterson, OSF, 'The Third Order Tradition of Evangelical Life' in *Vita Evangelica, Essays in Honour of Margaret Carney, OFS*. USA: The Franciscan Institute, St Bonaventure University, 2006, p. 471.
21 J. P. Chinnici, OFM, in K. Moffatt, *FSM General Chapter Workshop PPT Presentation on Evangelical Life*, 2009.
22 I. Delio, 'Living in the Ecological Christ', in *Franciscan Studies*, 64, 2006, p. 477.
23 R. J. Armstrong, OFMCap., 'If My Words Remain in You. Foundations of the Evangelical Life', p. 72.
24 Cf. W. J. Short, OFM, *The Franciscans*. Delaware: Michael Glazier, 1989; R. Pazzelli, TOR, *The Franciscan Sisters*. Steubenville: Franciscan University Press, 1993; P. Peano, OFM, *Bearing Christ to the People: The Franciscan Sisters, Their Origins, History and Persisting Values*, 1996.
25 P. Rivi, *This is Me*, p. 15.
26 Pope Francis, *Angelus Address*, New Year's Day 2014.
27 J. P. Chinnici, OFM, 'Evangelical and Apostolic Tensions', p. 100.

28 J. Corriveau, OFMCap., 'Evangelical Brotherhood' *Circular Letter 11*. Rome, 1997, pp. 4–7.
29 W. J. Short, OFM, 'Give An Account of the Hope that Lies Within You', in *The Cord*, 53/5, 2003, pp. 252–9.
30 M. B. Ingham, 'The Logic of the Gift: Clare of Assisi and Franciscan Evangelical Life', in *The Cord*, 60/3, 2010, p. 252.
31 Ibid., pp. 252–3.
32 Ibid., p. 254.
33 *The Code of Canon Law*, Canon 674.
34 J. P. Chinnici, 'The Prophetic Heart: The Evangelical Form of Religious Life in Contemporary United States', in *The Cord*, 44/11, 1994, pp. 292–306.
35 *The Code of Canon Law*, Canon 578.
36 R. J. Armstrong et al, *Francis of Assisi, The Saint*, vol. 1, p. 125.
37 R. J. Armstrong et al, *Francis of Assisi, The Prophet*, vol. 3, p. 314.
38 J. P. Chinnici, OFM, 'Evangelical and Apostolic Tensions', p. 96.
39 J. McDonnell, OSF, *Growing Unto Christ. A Franciscan Response in Faith*. UK: Webberley Limited, 1988, p. 10.
40 Franciscan Sisters Minoress, *The Constitutions, The Spirit and Purpose of our Congregation*, p. 1.
41 Ibid.
42 Sacred Congregation for Institutes of Consecrated Life, *Essential Elements in Church Teaching on Religious Life*. Vatican, 1983.
43 D. Lapsanski, *Evangelical Perfection, An Historical Examination of the Concept in the Early Franciscan Sources*. USA: The Franciscan Institute, 1977, p. 289.
44 M. Blastic, OFM, 'Franciscans Doing Theology', Paper given at The National Franciscan Forum, Colorado Springs, and sponsored by the Franciscan Institute of St Bonaventure University, 1997, p. 83.
45 M. Higgins, OFM, 'Active-Contemplative Synthesis' in *The Cord*, 46/5, 1995, p. 34.
46 D. Lapsanski, *Evangelical Perfection*, p. 288.
47 Saint Clare, 'The Testament of Saint Clare', in *Francis and Clare, The Complete Works*. New York; Paulist Press, 1982, pp. 227–8.
48 Franciscan Federation Third Order Regular, *Response to the Lineamenta in the Light of the 1994 Synod of Bishops on Consecrated Life in the Church*.
49 T. Radcliffe, 'The Identity of Religious Today', 1996.
50 J. P. Chinnici, OFM, 'Evangelical and Apostolic Tensions', p. 101.

TOTAL GIFT

Chapter Four

Mystics and Prophets
Old and New

*These new forms of consecrated life now taking place
alongside the older ones bear witness to the constant
attraction which the total gift of self to the Lord
continues to exert on the present generation. They also
show how the gifts of the Holy Spirit complement one
another.*   (Vita Consecrata, 12)

When I reflect on Religious Life from its beginnings to
the present day, I am struck by the thread of continuity
and the dynamism of change that lie at the heart of our
way of life. At first glance these two characteristics may
seem to be at odds, but in fact they are absolutely
necessary for the survival of this gift in the Church. Vita
Consecrata assures us that 'In this newness the Spirit
does not contradict himself. Proof of this is the fact that
the new forms of consecrated life have not supplanted
the earlier ones'.[1] The well-known author, Christopher
Jamison, would go so far as to say that 'The future
depends on the possibility of dialogue between the old
and new Orders'.[2]

In this chapter I hope to give readers a taste of this
dialogue and the way in which the 'new' and also the
'renewed' older Orders have evolved as a result. For me
it has been a fascinating study and I continue to marvel

at the way in which the Holy Spirit of God moves among his people. I have familiarised myself with new groups and renewed groups by meeting with new Founders of Consecrated Life and where this was not possible I have relied on the websites of different groups which then led to further reading, research and questionnaires. The conclusions I present do not give the full picture but are limited by the context and purpose of this book and also by the wishes of those I have contacted.

Before presenting some characteristics of the new and the renewed older groups, I would like to reflect briefly on the analysis given by Fr Jamison where he offers the pros and cons of the new and the old, and the necessity of dialogue if both wish to survive. First, he says that Religious Life is like a wheel – people keep on reinventing it. He concludes that this is good and God-given because of the new life that it generates within the Church. However, there is a need for dialogue between the well-established Orders and new expressions of Religious Life because they need each other, the former to receive new life, the latter to avoid pitfalls that experience prevents, or at least mitigates.

The reasons for dialogue, which Jamison outlines, are very challenging for both the old and new. Both positive and negative aspects are mentioned and it requires deep listening and humility to face these realities. I would like to focus on 'experience' and 'new life'. According to Jamison, the older Orders have 'great liberty of spirit' because they are so deeply rooted in the essence of the Gospel, in well-tried traditions of prayer and in generous service to the Church and the world. They have experience. Looking at the history and rich traditions of well-established older Orders, these gifts to the Church and the world have borne abundant fruit for centuries. However, such 'liberty of spirit' can lead to the vice of pride, in the sense that the Brothers and Sisters may be tempted to say 'We know best'.[3]

> They believe that their longevity means they know what the spirit of the Religious Life is and entitles them to sit lightly to the letter of their Order's tradition – and, in some cases, sit lightly to the Catholic tradition. We know best.[4]

If the older Orders are tempted to pride and independence, a stance that can create groups 'with the Gospel redesigned and the Church marginalised', Jamison concludes that the newer Orders can 'fall into vanity and self-satisfaction'. Their fervour and zeal, optimism and trust in Divine Providence, their excessive reliance on rules and regulations, can give them a false security and even stunt authentic growth in their members. Consequently, Jamison asks how the old and the new can come together in humility and magnanimity. His conclusion is the need to recognise the Order's emerging charism.

Building on the reflections and challenges presented in the previous chapter on fidelity to the founding charism, it is obvious that a listening, humble, obedient and contemplative openness to the leading of the Holy Spirit is the foundation for creative fidelity to the Order's original inspiration, lived with integrity and prophetic newness. This emphasis on the mystical and the prophetic has always been at the heart of the call to Religious Life and they have been highlighted again in recent decades. If adhered to, the call to mystical encounter and prophetic witness will safeguard both the new and old in their desire to be 'creatively faithful'.

New Congregations

From the research I have done in preparation for this chapter, it is obvious that new Congregations and Associations of Consecrated Life place great emphasis on private and communal prayer, life shared in and with others in community, common apostolates, visible witness by wearing distinctive clothing and a very clear sense of identity and charism. These are consistent with the research presented by Cathy Jones from the National Vocations Office. She states:

> Those entering apostolic congregations (both male and female) are practically all doing so in congregations where the majority (and often all) the members live in community and have a rhythm of communal prayer. Therefore, considering vocational 'choice' from a purely human perspective, clarity of function or specificity of role, as well as communal life and common prayer, are clearly significant influences.[5]

The following are a few examples from the completed questionnaires relating to the charism and the original inspiration and/or perceived need that prompted a new group of Religious in the Church at this time. These represent Dominican, Franciscan and Carmelite spiritualities and their new initiatives cover three decades. What is significant is the fact that these new groups adopt and adapt an existing spirituality, bringing to life the Word of God which says, 'Every scribe who becomes a disciple of the kingdom of Heaven is like a house-holder who brings out from his storehouse new things as well as old' (Mt 13:52). Respecting the individual groups, I have preserved anonymity except for the particular spirituality each has embraced. These are only a small sample of many Congregations that have been founded within the last fifty years. Some responded but did not want to be included in this publication.

1. **Founded in 1988, USA.** We were founded to renew the contemplative dimension of the Franciscan form of life with charisms of Crucified Love, Mercy, Poverty and Contemplation. We felt called to emphasise the contemplative life and to do works of mercy like the early Franciscans (contemplative but not cloistered).

   Here we have a clear sense of identity: spirituality, charism and mission; living the vows of poverty, chastity and obedience; common life; common and individual prayer with common celebration of the Eucharist as the source and summit of our life; vibrant fraternal/community interaction; common apostolate. The Sisters wear a religious habit.

   Number of Sisters 36.

2. **Founded in 1994, UK.** We were formed as a new Congregation within the Dominican Order as a result of a different understanding and vision for carrying out our life – with a return to monastic observance (silence, enclosure, habit, sung office) and the common life. Our particular charism is preaching and teaching the Faith.

   Number of Sisters 11.

3. **Founded 2004, UK.** Our charism is vocational, Incarnational and Marian. It is about enabling people to live vocationally by responding to the call of love in their lives and helping them to grow in the freedom to make well-discerned choices. The emerging charism with its unique blend of prayer, community and mission prompted the start of this new community nourished by Carmelite spirituality. What attracts young people today are such elements as community life, prayer in common, especially chanting the Divine Office, Eucharistic adoration and daily Mass, love for the Church and the Pope, a contemplative/active balance, the relatively young age of the community, newness, a welcoming atmosphere, joy and our model of formation. Our website and Facebook page give information as well as inspiration.

Number of Sisters 6

Perhaps some of these characteristics are partly what Jamison refers to as externals, but such distinctive characteristics have identified Religious Life for generations. So what is new?

To try to answer this question we would need to mention briefly, not the changes, but one of the *effects* of the changes that have happened, especially in apostolic Religious Institutes since Vatican II. In a recent publication Cathy Jones refers to the confusion young people have today when they are trying to discern their possible call to Religious Life. It would appear that the confusion arises from a 'lack of clarity about its own particularity'. The author states, 'The comparison of active Religious Life with other forms of consecrated life has demonstrated that the lived expression of many apostolic religious is hard to distinguish from secular consecration.'[6] In other words, the distinguishing features of the new Institutes referred to above are no longer applicable to many older active Institutes today. It would seem that the new Institutes are reclaiming much that was lost or discarded by older Institutes of Religious Life in recent decades. It is not the purpose of this chapter to look at the pros and cons of what has happened in the past fifty years. My intention is to explore Religious Life both in its newer forms and also in well-established forms in relation to religious identity.

My conclusion is that Religious Life, whether old or new, is essentially mystical and prophetic. How then are we going to nurture, develop and rekindle this tradition in both old and new Orders? That can only be answered by each Order because this expression will be dependent upon era, culture and charism. Such diversity is the gift of the Holy Spirit, but what is essential is that each Institute knows with clarity and conviction, first the particularity of the gift of Religious Life and then the particularity of its expression within a given charism. However, underpinning both mysticism and prophecy is the total self-gift of the person to Jesus. It is what Ruth Burrows refers to as 'the ground level' of Religious Life. 'It is the daily intention and effort to live for God alone and not at all for ourselves'.[7]

From the questionnaires, interviews and research I have undertaken, I am drawn to make a parallel with words spoken by Pope Francis on the Feast of the

Presentation of Our Lord and the celebration of this as a Feast of Consecrated Life. During his homily Pope Francis stressed the importance of the encounter with Jesus and also the distinction between the young and the old, which we celebrate in this Feast. His words are worth quoting at length.

> And in the consecrated life we live the encounter between the young and the old, between observation and prophecy. Let's not see these as two opposing realities! Let us rather allow the Holy Spirit to animate both of them, and a sign of this is joy: the joy of observing, of walking within a rule of life; the joy of being led by the Spirit, never unyielding, never closed, always open to the voice of God that speaks, that opens, that leads us and invites us to go towards the horizon. It's good for the elderly to communicate their wisdom to the young; and it is good for the young people to gather this wealth of experience and wisdom, and to carry it forward, not so as to store it in a museum, but to bring it forward addressing the challenges of life, to carry it forward for the sake of respective religious orders and of the whole Church.[8]

In the context of personal growth and maturity for the sake of the Kingdom and the mission of Jesus, there are particular invitations and challenges in these words of Pope Francis. Unpacking and understanding them is crucial for the future of Religious Life both old and new, and our call from Pope Francis to 'be men and women who are able to wake up the world'.[9]

New groups of Religious are mostly people in the first half of life. Their needs are different from older

Religious in well-established Orders. However, there are also younger people entering older established Orders, so what are the needs of 'the younger generation' in Religious Life, be they in old or new Orders? Pope Francis refers to the joyful observance of the law by the youthful Mary and her husband Joseph when they presented the Infant Jesus in the Temple. He also speaks of the wisdom of the elderly prophets, Simeon and Anna. These two wise, prophetic elders are full of life because they are filled and animated by the Holy Spirit, obedient to his action and sensitive to his calls. Pope Francis concludes that observance of the law and prophecy are not opposed. They need each other.

A number of other new foundations did not wish to be part of this study but the information gleaned from their websites would suggest that they share the characteristic features mentioned above. In this context I am aware of the needed balance between observance and wisdom. And from my own experience of thirty years in the ministry of formation, I know that those who are starting out on their journey in Religious Life need and appreciate certain structures and observances to help them at this particular stage of their formation. However, rules and observances are not ends in themselves; rather they support the growth and maturity which formation facilitates. To quote Pope Francis again: 'Formation is a work of art, not a police action'.[10]

Older Renewed Orders

It would seem that there are some older well-established Orders, especially in America, that are now flourishing.

They had years when vocations were few in number but now they are thriving. In one case the Sisters receive twenty plus new entrants each year and this has gone on for several years. 'Research shows that those institutes of active Religious Life which are attracting new members have a clear identity and purpose precisely as being religious and not secular'.[11] In the United Kingdom also, statistics reveal that there is a rise in the number of vocations, but the monastic/contemplative Orders seem to attract more entrants than the active apostolic Orders because of their distinctive features. The following is a specific example of an older Order attracting new members today.

Founded in 1860, USA.
We are a contemplative-apostolic community in the spirit of St Dominic. As Dominicans, our charism is to contemplate and give to others the fruits of our contemplation. Thus we live a regular life with a monastic framework, while engaging in an active apostolate of teaching, evangelisation and other charitable works. We live a community life in religious houses which are centred in the Eucharist, praying, taking meals and recreating in common daily. Though we are not an enclosed cloistered community, we do observe within our houses a form of cloister that is appropriate to our contemplative-apostolic life, and to a life of religious observance in community.

We find that young people are drawn to a life of sacrifice and self-giving, love for Christ and the

Church and devotion to the Blessed Virgin Mary. They are attracted by the joy they find in the Sisters and in the community; by our liturgical prayer together as well as private prayer before the Blessed Sacrament. They are drawn to the silence in our life, balanced by laughter and recreation. They are also drawn to the religious habit and its public witness to Christ.

Number of Sisters 295.

Overview

It is obvious that there are similarities between new communities and older communities that are flourishing. To the keen observer, the words of Pope Francis are timely and relevant regarding observance and wisdom. Observance of law in the context of youthful beginnings, and wisdom and prophecy in the context of a later stage of the spiritual journey, are not opposed. We need both. Although we may transcend the need for 'observance' as we knew it at an earlier stage of the journey, we also include it as we move to the stage of wisdom and prophecy. The Franciscan author, Richard Rohr, when writing of spirituality for the two halves of life, speaks of at least two major tasks. The first he identifies with the first half of life, the task to build a strong 'container' or identity. The second, which he identifies with the second half of life, is to find the contents that the container is meant to hold. A deep understanding of this process is crucial in the art of formation both initial and on-going. This insight throws light on the emerging face of Religious Life in new Institutes, and also on the changing face and challenges older Orders confront – at both personal and communal levels – to embrace the second half of life tasks with a sense of adventure, enthusiasm, humour and Gospel boldness. The essence will always be rooted in a personal encounter with Jesus (mysticism), which leads to the thrilling and awesome discovery of one's true identity made fruitful in radical self-giving (prophecy).

Passion for Christ and Passion for Humanity

Exploring this radical self-giving, the International Congress on Consecrated Life, celebrated in Rome in 2004, chose the theme 'Passion for Christ and passion for humanity'. The Scripture texts were John 4:1–42 where Jesus meets the Samaritan woman at Jacob's well, and Luke 10:29–37, the parable of the Good Samaritan. These two biblical icons integrate the mystical and the prophetic in a way that highlights both adoration and compassion. Whether newly established or founded on centuries of tradition, adoration and compassion are woven into the fabric of Religious Life in its varied expressions and Spirit-given charisms.

In a recent address to Women Major Superiors, Pope Francis said, 'To adore and to serve: two attitudes that cannot be separated, but must always go hand in hand'.[12] I would like to develop these two themes in the light of the challenges facing Religious in the twenty-first century. Beginning this book in the Year of Faith, is perhaps a timely reminder that our way of life is born and nurtured in faith and a very personal, intimate and mystical encounter with the Jesus of the Gospels. Both

Pope Benedict and Pope Francis emphasise the importance of the personal encounter with Jesus Christ. For
me, this emphasis points to the mystical foundation of
Religious Life, without which total self-giving is impossible. This twin theme, mysticism and prophecy, was the
focus for the Major Superiors Conference in Rome in
2010.

From the personal mystical encounter emerges the call
to prophecy. Pope Francis has clearly stated that
'Religious Life is prophecy'.[13] This prophetic stance
makes demands of us and, at times, may cause tension;
but ultimately we acknowledge that our vocation is an
essential charism for the journey of the Church.

> It is not possible that a consecrated woman and a conse-
> crated man not 'feel' along with the Church … It is an
> absurd dichotomy to think of living with Jesus without
> the Church, of following Jesus outside of the Church, of
> loving Jesus without loving the Church.[14]

Challenging us to be in the Church and of the Church
and for the Church, I would like to spend a little time
reflecting on the implications for each Religious and
each Congregation, whether old or new, to respond to
the invitation to be both mystical and prophetic in the
twenty-first century. Speaking to the International
Union of Superiors General in 2013, Pope Francis
proclaimed this same message by likening Religious Life
to an 'exodus', exhorting Major Superiors to 'Help your
communities to live the "exodus" from the self on a
journey of adoration and service, above all through the
three pillars of your life (i.e. the vows)'. We could use the

words adoration and service interchangeably with mysticism and prophecy. I will try to unpack the implications of both as this chapter unfolds.

The Call to be a Mystic

As a follower of St Francis of Assisi, I am aware that he was both a mystic and a prophet in a way that has changed the Church and world through the centuries. From the beginning of his mystical experience with Jesus Crucified in the broken-down church of San Damiano, and his mystical encounter on the road with Christ in the leper, through to his mystical encounter and total identification with Christ Crucified on Mount La Verna, Francis's intimacy with God was part and parcel of his everyday loving and living. In and through all these everyday encounters, Francis rebuilt the Church of God in a very practical way as founder, prophet and saint. Whether Institutes of Consecrated Life are old or new, 'mysticism and prophecy belong to the genetic codes of our ecclesial identity and our mission for the Kingdom of God'.[15] And yet according to another speaker at the same Major Superiors Conference, there is a felt need and a real challenge to rekindle and revive the mystico-prophetic tradition.

> In this twenty-first century where present models of religious life are changing and new models clearly demonstrating this mystico-prophetic tradition are still not evident, the challenge for each of us is to enflesh in our daily lives the practical aspects of being mystical and prophetic'.[16]

This enfleshing of the mystical and prophetic resonates particularly with the experiences of St Francis of Assisi. Ever practical and concrete in fulfilling the Will of God, Francis had numerous significant mystical experiences throughout his life, but a constant characteristic was this practical application to his encounter with Christ. For example, during his mystical encounter with the Crucified Christ in the broken-down church of San Damiano, Francis was invited to rebuild the Church of God, which was falling into ruin. Interpreting this to mean the physical church of San Damiano, Francis set to his rebuilding programme immediately. Only later did he fully understand the implications of the message and its challenge for the entire People of God. Similarly with his meeting the leper. Francis, in reaching out as a brother to the poorest and least in the society of his day, encountered the broken Body of Christ. From that time onwards, whenever Francis met a leper or a poor person, he met the poor, crucified Christ. This is mysticism in its most concrete, practical expression, rooted in the intimacy of love of God and one's neighbour.

To reach such intimacy requires grace and discipline, an intense awareness of the need for daily conversion of heart in the struggle with the false self and its attachments. Such integrity and purity of heart is costly. Deep listening to the Word of God and a faith-filled personal response in loving service is the only way to nurture the mystic-prophetic vocation. When I look at the life of Francis of Assisi, I see clearly the power and fruitfulness of this calling. And I too feel called, challenged and inspired to enter more deeply into the mystery.

A mystic, then, is one who shows the rest of us who we really are, who we can become, if only we would realize the gift of God that is already within us and respond in our concrete daily lives to God's great gift of love. The mystic shows us how not to let God's word return to God empty. The mystic uncovers the mystery, a mystery inside each one of us, and models what it looks like and what it accomplishes.[17]

When individuals become mystics and prophets, then we can look forward to mystical and prophetic Congregations. Reflecting on the beginnings of the Franciscan Family, it is obvious that it was not just Francis and Clare who were the mystics and prophets. No, the sisters and brothers who lived with Francis and Clare also shared uniquely and abundantly in these same gifts through their love for Christ, the Church and the world, and in their interaction and sharing with each other. We too, in our respective Religious families also share in the charism of our founding fathers and mothers. Consequently we can set the world on fire, as did they in and for their time. The challenge is no less great now.

I have learned, from walking with Francis and Clare, that mystical experience usually precedes prophetic action and proclamation of the Good News of the Gospel. The importance of deep listening to the Word of God, allowing it to inform, reform and transform one's heart is a prerequisite for authentic prophetic action. It was not an easy journey for St Francis who repeatedly embraced the desert encounter with the living God, purifying his heart in the furnace of love. Then and only then could he read the signs of the times in the lives of his brothers and sisters, especially the most marginalised, and respond courageously. It is the same for us. We too are called to a mysticism that will prepare us to be prophetic witnesses, first within our own time and place, and then further afield if called to this by God. This is where personal vocation and Congregational charisms inform, guide, challenge, inspire and empower needed change with a freshness and creativity that is a reflection of the self-giving, self-emptying, abundant life of God – Father, Son and Holy Spirit.

The Call to be a Prophet

If we are faithful to our call and lovingly embrace mysticism and its transforming action in our hearts, we will be led to respond to the needs of the contemporary world in which we live. As I have already stated, Pope Francis has asked Religious to wake up the world. That is what prophets have always been called to do. Pope Francis has even encouraged us to make a loud noise about it if we need to! Our task now is to recognise and respond to the particular way in which we are called to be prophetic within our own time, place, culture and charism. 'There are seeds of the future which can still sprout from our roots, no matter how old they are'.[18] This is the meaning of creative fidelity referred to in *Vita Consecrata* but, to rise to this challenge requires both faith and vision. Faith in the gift we have received and vision to interpret it for our present history. To do this it may be helpful to ponder the experiences of the prophets of the Old Testament, especially the experience of the prophet Jeremiah.

Comparing our present experience in Religious Life to

that of the prophet Jeremiah, the Carmelite author, Bruno Secondin, challenges us to look at our heritage and face the reality of our present situation. We have a choice to make regarding our responses, and choices have consequences, not only for ourselves but also for the wider family of humanity.

> Like Jeremiah, we can also multiply the desperate confessions, full of bitterness and helpless rebellion. Or else, precisely like the resistant Jeremiah, we can think over the roots of our own adventure, the founding experience that gave a start to everything. Yes, it was not we who invented our charism, nor the mission to build and uproot, to destroy and to plant, to cry out and to intercede. The Lord gave and consecrated right from the start ... we must rediscover the radiance of the original experience.[19]

I am reminded of an occasion in the life of St Francis when the state of the Order in general, and the behaviour of some of the friars in particular, were a cause of deep sorrow and grief to him. Things were not as they used to be in the beginning and this was a heavy cross to bear. But in prayer, the Lord drew him to a deeper understanding of himself and the Order. Greater detachment and greater trust were called for and Francis rose to the challenge. The humanity of the situation is quite humorous. The Lord said to Francis, 'Why are so upset, little man? Have I set you up over my religion so that you can forget that I am its main protector'.[20]

The experience of the prophet Jeremiah and the experience of Francis of Assisi can speak to our present experience of Religious Life, especially in the western world. The challenge is to rediscover the original experience by opening ourselves to the transforming power of the crucified and risen Christ, our Lord and Master, our Teacher and our Bridegroom. Jesus said 'Follow Me', and this we do by embracing the path of both crucifixion and resurrection. The mystical encounter with Jesus unites us in a very real way with the whole of human experience – joy, sorrow, agony, ecstasy and everything in between in the ordinary lived experience of every day. This should lead to prophecy and proclamation. But first we need solidarity with Jesus, the Way, the Truth and the Life, and in him with our brothers and sisters on the journey of life. This was the path taken by our Founders and Foundresses. This is what we are called to do in our own time and in our own way. The essence is the same. It is the call to follow Christ, crucified and risen, grounded and expressed in personal vocation and Congregational charism.

On the journey to maturity we will have to face and pass through many 'dark nights' of the soul. Personally and communally, we can resist this tremendous grace of growth and purification and look for all kinds of reasons to explain our present difficulties, or we can embrace our present situation with bold confidence, generous love and courageous perseverance. At the outset, I focused on faith and perhaps as we approach the Year of Consecrated Life, we can step out anew in faith where the Spirit beckons.

In our present climate of advanced technology, we are very much aware of the global scene that touches our hearts on a daily basis. Needs abound. It is possible to feel overwhelmed by the sheer immensity of unrelieved suffering. Yet, even Jesus could only respond to what was before his eyes. Creative fidelity to our charism will determine our response both near and far. And in our own Minoress Congregation, as a very small part of the wider Franciscan family, we are very much aware 'that the choice of "little things" and "little people" is characteristic of God's dealings with humanity'.[21] We often remind ourselves of those beautiful words in Deuteronomy: The Lord set His heart on you and chose you not because you were the most numerous of all peoples – for indeed you were the smallest of all – but because He loved you' (7:7). Therefore, we joyfully embrace the truth that God acts in the small and the ordinary as well as in the great and the extraordinary. Consequently, we move forward, usually talking small but courageous steps (see below) to witness to the Reign of God.

Love of God and love of our brothers and sisters is the last will and testament of Jesus. Whether we use terms like prayer and service, adoration and compassion, active and contemplative, mysticism and prophecy, it is obvious that there is an intimate and essential relationship between love of God and love of neighbour. It is not a case of either/or, but of both/and, which makes the Good News of the Gospel a joyful reality in daily living and loving. This became very apparent to me during one of our recent Congregational General Chapters. When reviewing our history since the previous Chapter, we celebrated the completion of two small but significant and courageous projects: The Portiuncula, a House of Prayer and Solitude in Derbyshire, and also a facility in South Africa to feed, educate, and support poor, hungry and needy children and their families. These are not world-shattering ventures but small steps born of love where Divine Providence has placed us.

How important then to return to our founding inspiration. Just as St Francis, when visited with Divine favours in his many mystical encounters, quickly put into practice the love he received by ministering to his brothers and sisters on the road of life, we too are called to do the same. The manner of service may differ, but the mission with and for the reign of God in this world is as real today as in the beginning. 'Consecrated life is ... essentially consecration to Christ (mysticism) and proclamation of the Good News (prophecy)'.[22] Pope Francis reiterated this same message when he met with the Superiors General, saying that a radical approach is required of all Christians, but religious persons are called upon to follow the Lord in a special way. 'Consecrated life is prophecy. God asks us to fly the nest and to be sent to the frontiers of the world, avoiding the temptation to "domesticate" them. This is the most concrete way of imitating the Lord'.[23] Jesus says: 'Follow Me'. This is an invitation to keep moving where the Spirit leads, so that our present epoch may be redeemed and transformed according to the plan and action of God – not us! 'Being with Jesus shapes a contemplative approach to history which knows how to see and hear the presence of the Spirit everywhere'.[24]

Called to walk the wounded path of human history, we continue to follow Jesus and carry forward the plan of God until Christ is all in all. This is not a human work. It is the work of the Holy Spirit who propels us forward if we surrender to his action within us and within human history. Called individually to be in communion with others, we are co-creators with God for the life of the world. This has always been the dynamic of Religious Life but it takes a mystic and a prophet to see with the eyes of the heart and respond with the power of the Spirit. 'We must entrust ourselves to the Spirit's action which departs from the intimacy of hearts, manifests itself in communion and spreads itself in mission'.[25] Attentive, obedient listening in faith, and tender, compassionate action in love, bring consolation and liberation in true Jubilee celebration.

If mysticism and prophecy are the dynamic qualities of consecrated life, then our present challenge is to nurture the process that makes these a reality. Pope Francis has already reminded us that Religious Life is not about a culture of management and marketing, leading to the worship of false idols and values, rather it is living according to the wisdom of the Beatitudes, an authentic following of Christ; hence the emphasis on 'living differently'.

We have already spoken about the Transfiguration of Jesus as the chosen icon of Consecrated Life. Perhaps the relevance of this event becomes even clearer when we speak of the mystic-prophetic call. Therefore I would like to return to the Transfiguration within the context of mysticism and prophecy. We have already referred to the twofold experience of being *on* the mountain and coming down *from* the mountain. It is not easy to hold these two realities together but that is what we are called to do, starting within our own hearts before we touch the hearts of others. This formation of the heart would seem to be a prerequisite for any meaningful, fruitful and creative fidelity to the prophetic call. 'Only the mystic is a prophet and all prophets must be mystics'.[26] No matter how busy or urgent the needs are, we are encouraged to 'cultivate the contemplative dimension, even amid the whirlwind of more urgent and heavy duties'.[27]

In the mountaintop experience of mysticism, our encounter with Jesus transfigured takes us ever more deeply into the mystery of the Trinity, the source of life, love and mission. In the Transfiguration we are caught up in the mystery of the passion, death and resurrection of Jesus. In the intimacy of that experience, we hold and face within us both light and darkness, disfiguration and transfiguration. Strengthened in faith, we, like the apostles, come down from the mountain, longing to journey with our brothers and sisters from all forms of disfiguration to transfiguration. But if this 'insight of faith is lacking, life itself loses meaning, the faces of brothers and sisters are obscured and it becomes impossible to recognise the face of God in them. Historical events remain ambiguous and deprived of hope'.[28]

The Gospel challenge of Franciscan Evangelical Life is deeply rooted in our on-going personal experience of discovering what St Francis discovered when he said: 'Consider, O human being, in what great excellence the Lord God has placed you, for He created and formed you to the image of His beloved Son according to the body and to His likeness according to the Spirit'.[29] Wherever humanity is disfigured by suffering and injustice in any form, there we wish to bring the comfort, compassion and consolation of God. Recognising each person as brother and sister creates communion and fraternity, that family atmosphere where each one is cherished, nurtured, valued and accepted.

One of the great signs that every consecrated life can offer as a poor and evangelical sign is simply the home: that wherever consecrated people live, there is a house that is open, welcoming, caring as a sign of the communion of the Church.[30]

The same author warns that we can only humanise our culture and our society if we first humanise the members of our own communities. Again it is Pope Francis who urges us to create and build communities where each person can grow in love, responsibility, freedom and fidelity. Tenderness is good for us, and communities are places where we experience the gift of love and festive freedom in joy. This joy is a gift of the Holy Spirit. 'A joyless community is one that is dying out'.[31] He does not ignore or minimise the problems and conflicts that can arise but he invites us to 'caress conflicts' when they arise in community. This is the language of familial tenderness, which begins with those we live with and extends to those with whom we journey in our varied ministries and service.

Focusing on the ordinary everyday experiences as we relate to God and to one another demystifies both mysticism and prophecy. While 'contemplation expands into prophetic aptitude'[32] we realise that both need to be properly understood, nurtured, lived according to the charism we have inherited.

Within the gifted multiplicity of charisms within Religious Life, we Consecrated Religious, as a group, are called anew to wake up the world. Each Institute must explore this invitation with hearts attentive to the uniqueness of our legacy. However, there is a shared foundational level and shared vision emphasised by Pope Francis who wants us to be prophetic by the way we live. Live differently. Live simply. Live authentically. Be brother, be sister to every person we meet, becoming travelling companions and sharing in the struggles that face us in this twenty-first century, finding new ways to reach out and walk with others on the journey of life. What is new for each Religious and each Institute will depend on the personal vocation of each person and the shared charism that distinguishes the group. Discovery of this is no small task and challenge. It is not for the faint-hearted.

In the next chapter by way of example I would like to turn to Francis and Clare of Assisi. They did something new that revolutionised the understanding of Religious Life as it was then known, which in turn impacted on society, the Church and the world at large. We are called to do the same.

Reflection

As a member of a Religious Community, do you accept that new life, new vision, renewal and change begin with *you*. How do you nurture and respond to the privilege and responsibility of being both a mystic and prophet?

Notes

1   Pope John Paul II, *Vita Consecrata*, 12.
2   C. Jamison, 'The future depends on the possibility of dialogue between the old and new Orders', in *The Tablet*, April 2012, p. 5.
3   Ibid.

4 Ibid.

5 C. Jamison, OSB, (ed.), *Theologies of Vocation From Scripture to the Present Day*. London: Bloomsbury, 2013, p. 143.

6 Ibid., p. 152.

7 R. Burrows, OCD, *Essence of Prayer*. London: Burns & Oates, 2006, p. 197.

8 Pope Francis, *Address to the Union of Superiors General*, Rome, May 2013.

9 Pope Francis, *The Union of Male Superiors General, 82nd General Assembly*, Rome, 2013.

10 Pope Francis, *Address to the Union of Superiors General*, Rome, May 2013.

11 C. Jamison, OSB, (ed.), *Theologies of Vocation From Scripture to the Present Day*, p. 152.

12 Pope Francis, *Address to the Union of Superiors General*, Rome, May 2013.

13 Ibid.

14 Ibid.

15 B. Secondin, O.Carm., 'The Almond Branch and the Boiling Pot (Jer. 1:11–13). What is the Future for our Mystical-Prophetic Heritage?', *UISG Address*, Rome, 2010.

16 J. Malone, CND, 'Demystifying Mysticism and Prophecy', *UISG Address*, Rome, 2010.

17 M. Bodo, OFM, *St Francis the Practical Mystic*, http://www.americancatholic.org/features/special Date of Access, 22/10/14.

18 B. Secondin, O Carm., 'The Almond Branch and the Boiling Pot (Jer. 1:11–13). What is the Future for our Mystical-Prophetic Heritage?', *UISG Address*. Rome, 2010.

19 Ibid.

20 R. J. Armstrong, OFMCap,, W.J.A. Hellmann, OFMConv,, W. J. Short, OFM, *Francis of Assisi, The Founder, Early Documents*, vol, 2. London, New York: New City Press, 2000, p. 349.

21 J. Cardinal Ratzinger, *God and the World*. San Francisco: Ignatius Press, 2002, p. 213.

22 C. Garcia, OCD, 'Mysticism and Prophecy. A Style of Life and New Areopagus', *Plenary Assembly of UISG*, Rome, 2010.

23 Pope Francis, *The Union of Superiors General, 82nd General Assembly*, Rome, 2013.

24 Pope Francis, *Rejoice! A Message from the teachings of Pope Francis. A Letter to Consecrated Men and Women in Preparation for the Year Dedicated to Consecrated Life.* London: CTS, 2014, p. 25.

25 Pope John Paul II, *Consecrated Life in the Third Millennium, Starting Afresh from Christ.* London, CTS, 2002, p. 27.

26 C. Garcia, OCD, 'Mysticism and Prophecy. A Style of Life and New Areopagus', *Plenary Assembly of UISG*, Rome, 2010.

27 Pope Francis, *Rejoice! A Message from the Teachings of Pope Francis. A Letter to Consecrated Men and Women in Preparation for the Year Dedicated to Consecrated Life.* London: CTS, 2014, p. 25.

28 Ibid.

29 R. J. Armstrong, OFMCap, *et al, Francis of Assisi, Early Documents*, vol, 1, p. 131.

30 C. Garcia, OCD, 'Mysticism and Prophecy. A Style of Life and New Areopagus', *Plenary Assembly of UISG*, Rome, 2010.

31 Pope Francis, *Rejoice! A Message from the Teachings of Pope Francis,* p. 33.

32 Ibid., p. 25.

NEW every MORNING

Chapter 5

Infinite Horizons

We fear that God may force us to strike out on new paths and leave behind our all too narrow, closed and selfish horizons in order to become open to his own.

(Pope Francis)

Infinite horizons or closed horizons, the choice is ours. Both are open to us. Saints in every age teach us how to engage in a holy newness that radiates total originality and beauty. Theirs is the infinite horizon that trusts new paths as the Holy Spirit dictates. Francis and Clare of Assisi were among this number and they continue to serve as attractive examples of radical Gospel living. We too, in this twenty-first century are called to a holy newness, rooted in the revealed Word of God, and ultimately in the Word, Jesus Christ, the Rock of our salvation, our Way, our Truth and our Life.

Newness in Sacred Scripture

The theme of newness is expressed in many different ways in Scripture. We have examples of a new heart, a new covenant, new wine, new wineskins, new teaching, new revelations, a new commandment, a new creation, a new man, a new Jerusalem, a new heaven, a new earth, a new birth, new life and New Testament. This is a profound and exciting aspect of biblical revelation.

When we encounter the God-man, Jesus Christ, then we have experiential knowledge of 'holy newness' and 'new horizons'. The encounter is central. 'Being Christian is not the result of an ethical choice or a lofty idea, but the encounter with an event, a person, which gives life a new horizon and a decisive direction'.[1] It is beyond the scope and purpose of this book to deal with every aspect of newness mentioned above. For present purposes, my concentration will be on a new heart and a new commandment, with special relevance to our present situation in Religious Life because these refer directly to our call to mysticism and prophecy.

A New Heart

As I have mentioned elsewhere, heart is one of the most used words in Scripture.[2] In the biblical sense it is so rich and varied in meaning, it almost defies definition. Here we are speaking of the most profound and complex inner mystery of what it means to be a person, and the person *par excellance* is Jesus Christ, God made man. 'It is impossible to find in the New Testament a word which more readily and accurately, more profoundly and with more human warmth, could come close to a definition of the Person of Christ than his Heart'.[3]

In responding to the call to be mystics, we are invited to a deep and personal encounter with the Person of Jesus Christ. In so doing we participate in the very life of the Trinity and become 'schools of prayer' for our brothers and sisters, who hunger for a deeper experience of God. In Franciscan parlance, we speak of making accessible to others the experience of God. We cannot do this unless we ourselves have been given a 'new heart', open, receptive, welcoming, warm, tender and compassionate, like the Heart of Jesus. He has revealed his heart through his teaching and example. In him word and deed are one and the same. 'The external signs, His parables and discourses, His whole life, as presented in the Gospels ... are not totally understood or understandable in all their profound meaning unless they are read from the angle of His heart'.[4] To make this point obvious, Pedro Arrupe states that Jesus, in describing himself, put aside all other metaphors and chose the heart as the revelation of his deepest sentiments and which we can imitate: 'Learn from Me, for I am gentle and humble of heart' (Mt 11:29). This focus on the heart brings Jesus very close as a fellow traveller on the human journey, one like us in every way, except sin.

In a previous chapter I reflected on the spousal nature of Religious Consecration. It seems to me that the symbol of the heart leads naturally to the biblical image of the bride and bridegroom. It is the language of intimacy and union. It is the indwelling of which St John speaks in his Gospel (Jn 15:4). Only such heart knowledge, experienced and shared, has the power to attract others to Christ. 'Why has so much of Christian history settled for a courtroom instead of a bridal chamber? It is really quite disturbing how this has corrupted the whole Gospel'.[5] What a challenge lies in these words! To centre our lives on love 'received new' every morning, is symbolised by the heart and all it evokes. 'Surely Yahweh's mercies are not over, His deeds of faithful love not exhausted; every morning they are renewed; great is His faithfulness' (Lam 3:23). Love is the heart of the Gospel message. Only love lasts forever. It is the foundation and unchanging truth that fulfils all desire, and is the key to understanding the origin, purpose and destiny of every human life. Such love without bounds, whose horizons are infinite, is indeed a 'new' commandment.

A New Commandment

When Jesus gave us a 'new' Commandment, he surpassed all understanding of the Old Testament commandments to love God and our neighbour as ourselves. He surpassed it by fulfilling it in himself; becoming God incarnate among us, and manifesting the love that lies at the heart of the Trinity. 'This is the revelation of God's love for us, that God sent his only Son into the world that we might have life through him' (1 Jn 4:9). This life is a life of love, freely given, unconditional in nature, total in self-giving, even to the point of death, and life-giving to the point of resurrection and transformation into a 'new creation' in Christ. What an overwhelming gift! And Jesus identifies this Commandment as his very own. 'This is my Commandment: love one another as I have loved you' (Jn 15:12). We can do what he has done. We can love with the love that is in the Heart of the Trinity. It is his gift that we, in our turn, may usher in the reign of God. 'It is by your love for one another that everyone will recognise you as my disciples' (Jn 13:35).

The 'new' Commandment to love is our God-given

ability to love with an all-inclusive and fraternal love. 'Love is now no longer a mere "command"; it is the response to the gift of love with which God draws near to us'.[6] The length and the breadth, the height and the depth of such love, while being beyond all human imagining, is also very practical and down-to-earth. Love of God and love of others are not two separate loves. They are two sides of the same coin. Such universal love is indeed revolutionary, a 'new' teaching, recognised by those who first listened to Jesus but just as difficult to accept now as it was then. As Pope Benedict points out, 'Despite being extended to all humanity, it is not reduced to a generic, abstract and undemanding expression of love, but calls for my own practical commitment here and now'.[7] These sentiments are reflected in our Congregational Constitutions, where we quote the Gospel of St Matthew, 'As long as you did it for one of these, the least of my brothers, you did it for me' (Mt 25:40). Since the beginning, a characteristic of Franciscan Evangelical life in the world was to do works of mercy, caring for others with the tenderness of God'.

Unless and until we move from a very narrow and selfish understanding of God's amazing, unconditional and universal love, our horizons will be restricted and limited. Much will depend on the depth of our relationship with Jesus, our level of spiritual maturity, our courage in dying to our small false self and its concerns, and our willingness to embrace the Good News in all its freshness and newness. This requires ever deeper and continuous immersion in both the death and resurrection of Jesus, which is inherent in Religious Consecration. Such on-going participation in the Paschal

Mystery is the source and foundation for 'new' life in
Christ.

> Upon the sacramental basis of Baptism in which it is
> rooted, religious profession is a new 'burial in the death
> of Christ': new, because it is made with awareness and
> by choice; new, because of love and vocation; new, by
> reason of unceasing 'conversion'. This 'burial in death'
> causes the person 'buried together with Christ' to '*walk
> like Christ in newness of life.*'[8]

God is always making all things new, and one of those
who embraced this truth with passion and personal
integrity was Francis of Assisi.

Francis and Newness

Celano, the first biographer of St Francis, puts before us
in a striking manner the unexpected newness and
renewal which came to birth in the Church and the
world, in the person of Francis. It is interesting that
Celano uses both words: 'new' and 'renewal'. They are
not the same reality though they are intimately
connected. Perhaps Richard Rohr sums it up succinctly
when he says: 'Both Jesus and Francis did not let the old
get in the way of the new but, like all religious geniuses,
revealed what the old was saying all along'.[9] This is the
perennial challenge. In one sense there is nothing new
under the sun, and in another sense each person in
his/her uniqueness, and each generation in its turn, has
to make the great discovery that in God everything is
eternally new! In Francis of Assisi we see how this
paradox is incarnated.

When Celano was commissioned by the Pope to write a life of Francis, in preparation for his Canonisation, Celano had an exceptionally difficult task to achieve. On the one hand he had to demonstrate that the holiness of Francis was in many ways similar to previously recognised Saints, and on the other hand he had to present Francis as a new kind of Saint, 'breaking with, surpassing or transcending the tradition'.[10] Usually the cult of the Saints relied heavily on the miraculous, evident during the person's life and also after his/her death. Although Celano eventually wrote a *Book of Miracles* demonstrating this aspect of Francis's holiness, and included some miracles in the biography for his canonisation, he emphasised virtue more than miracle, saying: 'We have not chosen to describe miracles – they do not make holiness but show it – but rather to describe the excellence of his life'.[11] As Bill Short points out, the recognition of miracles as complementary to the evidence provided by a virtuous life was somewhat of an innovation in the process of canonisation in the twelfth and early thirteenth centuries.[12]

This of course brings Francis very near to us and makes a 'holy newness' possible for all of us in our unique, and at the same time, very ordinary everyday lives. As Celano says, 'That is why every order, sex, and age finds in him a clear pattern of the teaching of salvation and an outstanding example of holy deeds'.[13]

Celano demonstrated that Francis was like other Saints before him, notably, St Anthony of Egypt, St Martin of Tours and St Augustine to name a few, and there were allusions to others Saints too throughout Celano's writings. Like Anthony of Egypt, when Francis heard the words of Jesus in the Gospel, inviting him to give away all his possession, he readily obeyed. This is exactly what St Athanasius records in the life of St Anthony of Egypt who became a model for Religious Life. Celano also likens Francis to the well-known St Martin of Tours, the soldier saint who gave his life to Christ and was an ardent follower of the Gospel. The words used by the biographer of Martin's life are exactly the same as those used by Celano, referring to Francis and the Gospel: 'For he was no deaf hearer of the Gospel'.[14] Francis is also compared to Augustine who searched for the will of God in the Scriptures. In the *Confessions* we read that he acted on what his eyes first saw when he opened the Scriptures. Celano says of Francis, 'He prayed earnestly that at the first opening of the book he would be shown what was best for him to do … In this he was led by the spirit of the saints and holy ones.'[15] Francis stands within the ancient tradition, following Christ according to the Gospel, and after the example of the Saints who preceded him. Yet, Francis also brought something completely new to the life of the Church and the world. This too, Celano clearly states, 'In these last times, a new Evangelist, like one of the rivers of Paradise, has poured out the streams of the Gospel in a holy flood over the whole world.'[16]

If, as Saint John Paul II said, 'Saints never grow old. They never become figures of the past, men and women of "yesterday". On the contrary, they are men and women of the future, witnesses of the world to come',[17] we may well ask: how is Francis a 'new' person, and what is the 'holy newness' the Church and the world experienced, and continues to experience, through him?

If we can understand and appreciate the 'new' that Francis brought, then we are in a better position to be renewed by his spirit and example. When individuals are faithful to grace and respond in love to their personal vocation, they are made whole and holy, and they inspire others to risk the same adventure in love. This is how new Institutes of Religious Life come to birth. An authentic and loving individual response to Christ, not only inspires and attracts others, but also invites others into the same experience of gifted newness. 'Many people, well-born and lowly, cleric and lay, driven by divine inspiration, began to come to Saint Francis, for they desired to serve under his constant training and leadership'.[18]

The fact that everyone felt included in Francis's new movement demonstrates the great reverence and respect Francis had for every individual. His emphasis on openness to, and acceptance of, the feminine in all forms of creation is very evident in his life and writings. Having embraced the challenge of integrating the masculine and feminine within himself, Francis showed a particular sensitivity and respect towards Clare. He recognised her unique call and contribution to his new movement in the Church. Such equality was concretely expressed in fraternity and in the mutual love and support, inspiration and encouragement the sisters gave to the brothers and *vice versa*. Brother/brother, sister/sister, brother/sister relationships were central in this new movement. Such equality did not reflect the hierarchical structure of the Church and society at that time.

We know that other forms of Religious Life existed at

the time of Francis but he chose none of these. Instead a
new form of Religious Life came into being through him.
This we have reflected on in a previous chapter, but for
our present purposes we highlight the 'new' aspects of
his way of life. It was considered a 'new' Order in the
Church. Celano tells us that Francis, the 'devoted father
instructed his new sons not so much in words and
speech but in deed and truth'.[19] Example speaks louder
than words, and in the case of Francis this is eminently
true. Poverty and humility, simplicity and joy were the
hallmarks of this new Order, founded on love, built on
love and lived in love, in response to him who first loved
us. 'What a great flame of charity burned in the new
disciples of Christ!'[20] It is this great love that characterises the life of Francis and is the foundation of his
becoming a completely new creation in and through and
with Christ.

Becoming a New Creation

Journeying into this newness means, in the first
instance, an attentive listening to the Word of God,
because the Word became flesh and lived among us. He
is the centre, the focus, the meaning and purpose, and
the example, *par excellence*, of how to become a 'new
creation' and renew the face the earth. Encountering the
self-emptying love of God in the humanity of Jesus, took
Francis into a whole new understanding of the humility
and lavishness of God, who became little and poor for
love's sake. So great was his appreciation of this great
mystery that he created a 'new' Bethlehem on the
hillside of Greccio. On that memorable occasion, Francis

recreated the conditions of that first Christmas and consequently 'simplicity is given a place of honour, poverty is exalted, humility is commended and out of Greccio is made a new Bethlehem'.[21] The re-enactment of the first Christmas had a profound effect on both the priest and the people. The priest enjoyed 'a new consolation' and the people were, 'ecstatic at this new mystery of new joy'.[22] The many references to 'new' in this scene reveal the effect Francis had on a world that had become oblivious to the mystery of the Incarnation. 'This innovative approach to depicting a theological mystery becomes an occasion for an outpouring of devotion'.[23]

Not only did Greccio become a 'new' Bethlehem, but Mount La Verna also became a 'new' Calvary. When Francis received the wounds of Christ in his hands, feet and side, he became a new saint unlike any other in history until that time. He was the first to bear in his body the wounds of Jesus. This caused the people to recognise that God had worked a new wonder in his servant Francis. 'A new miracle turned their minds to amazement'[24] because they had never witnessed anything like this before. 'This is a unique gift, a sign of special love' which led the people to give praise to God 'who gives new signs and works new wonders'.[25] He was a new Saint in that, in his very person, he was transformed into the likeness of the One he loved so passionately and so personally. That remains his call and invitation to each one of us: to respond to Love and to do what is ours to do.

From Greccio and La Verna, we can see how Francis witnessed in his own person to the simplicity, humility, poverty and love that was manifested in Jesus, God made man. In a world and a Church that was preoccupied with pomp and glory, honour and success, Francis preached the Gospel with his life, without judging or condemning in word or deed those who had lost the Gospel vision in their hearts. By his loving, countercultural stance, Francis awakened in peoples' hearts a spiritual renewal that continues to call forth new disciples. And one of his first and most faithful disciples was Clare, who in her own unique way, also brought a 'holy newness' to the world in which she lived.

Clare and Newness

When Thomas of Celano wrote the Life of Clare, he referred to that Spirit-filled moment in Clare's life when she heard of Francis, 'who like a new man, was renewing with new virtues the way of perfection forgotten by the world and she immediately desired to see and hear him'.[26] This she did, and her meetings with Francis led her to embrace the Gospel life and join the new movement of Francis and the brothers at the Portiuncula. This is how Celano describes that eventful day.

> This is the place in which a new army of the poor, under the leadership of Francis, took its joyful beginnings, so that it might be clearly seen that it was the Mother of Mercies, who brought to birth both Orders in her dwelling place.[27]

Clare described herself as '*la pianticella*', the little plant of the blessed Father Francis. At first sight this self-description might suggest that Clare did not have her own unique vocation and influence apart from Francis. Far from it! Clare, while understanding – perhaps more deeply than anyone else – the vision and charism of Francis's Gospel way of life, brought to the world her own 'holy newness' that had consequences not only for Religious Life, but also for the Church and the society in which she lived. Like Francis, she too emerges as a mystic and prophet, with an influence that remains ever attractive and ever new. 'It should not be surprising that a light so enkindled, so illuminating could not be kept from shining brilliantly and giving clear light in the house of the Lord'.[28]

In medieval times, society, the Church and Religious Life were founded on a hierarchical structure that reflected class distinctions relating to land, wealth, status and nobility of birth. Clare belonged to the nobility, and for her to reject the trappings that surrounded her way of life was perhaps even more astounding than Francis's rejection of status, wealth and power to which his merchant class were only aspiring. For both Francis and Clare, the encounter with Christ, poor and crucified, transformed their consciousness to such an extent that all stereotypes would give way to a new expression of Gospel living. Without the mystical encounter with Christ such radical living would not be possible. And in the light of our call to be mystics and prophets, it is with Clare's mystical encounter that I would like to begin this reflection on her 'holy newness'.

Clare the New Mystic

The mystical journey of Clare is very much like the journey of every person who desires deep union with God. It involves decision, desire, struggle, perseverance, suffering and joy – to name a few! The decision to follow Christ is rooted in our desire for loving union with him, but it is a costly endeavour because of our frail humanity, and must necessarily take us through the cross to glory. Clare knew this, and I find in her a real encouragement to persevere on the mystical journey, despite the obstacles on the way. This is what we mean by a life of penance, and it is written into our Franciscan Third Order Regular Rule of Life. 'Under the Lord's guidance, let them set out on a life of penance, knowing that we are all obliged to constant conversion of heart'.[29] This emphasis on the heart evokes not just a penitential austerity, but also an emphasis on love and the loving process of transformation that leads to union. Since Clare has been described as the woman with a warm and glowing heart, who ran after Christ, I simply wish to highlight here some aspects of newness that Clare presents as we journey into our own hearts and the heart of God.

Every new discovery of God's love is a new beginning, and each of us needs to discover our mystical roots. Clare, whom Pope Alexander IV described as 'This clear spring of the Spoleto Valley who furnished a new fountain of living water for the refreshment of souls,'[30] can show us the way to renew and refresh our lives in the power of the Holy Spirit who makes all things new. The heart, the symbol of love, has infinite horizons because love knows no bounds, and it is through contemplation of Jesus, that we enter more fully into the mystery of our transformation. This is the challenge Clare puts before us when she says:

> Place your mind before the mirror of eternity! Place your soul in the brilliance of glory! Place your heart in the figure of the Divine substance! And transform your entire being into the image of the Godhead Itself through contemplation.[31]

Like Francis, Clare realised that contemplation is the process of our remaking, of becoming a new creation. Let us discover what new teaching Clare proposes by her words and example.

A Crucified and Glorious Spouse

Most of us will be familiar with the ancient practice of *Lectio Divina*. There are four steps involved: reading, meditation, prayer and contemplation. For Clare, in her 'reading' of the San Damiano Crucifix, the final step is not contemplation but imitation. The steps she proposes are: gaze, consider, contemplate and imitate. Everything leads to imitation as the final goal. We become what we love. Clare, in gazing upon the Crucified and Glorious Christ, absorbed the mystery of lovingly holding humanity and divinity, heaven and earth, time and eternity within her own being. In so doing, Clare lived the mystery and became a teacher, a leader and a mirror for others. This she could do because she first gazed into Christ, the mirror where she learned through experience what the process of transformation involved.

The journey to maturity in Christ will take us, as it did Clare, through the stages of purification, enlightenment and union in mystical marriage. That is why we begin with Clare, gazing upon Jesus on the San Damiano Crucifix. 'The gaze on the Crucified Christ is an embrace of the heart ... by which the heart opens its arms to allow the Spirit of God's love to enter'.[32] And for me, the emphasis on the heart is central to my understanding of Clare's mysticism. I remember attending a course with novices from many different families of Franciscans. The Franciscan friar who was giving one of the talks asked us for our definition of poverty. There was a variety of answers but I remember giving just one word as my definition: space. His comment was 'Interesting!' I link 'space' with poverty because for me it means having an empty heart to receive the lavishness of God's generosity. I think this is what Clare discovered by gazing at the Crucified and Glorious figure of Christ on the San Damiano Cross. This is surely the connection with her amazing and new request for the 'Privilege of Poverty'. To live without rights, without possessions, without wealth, status, power and privilege was a new, creative and innovative reality in the Church in general, and in Religious Life in particular. It was a privilege not easily or quickly granted. But Clare was a determined and heroic woman and neither Popes nor Prelates could dissuade her from persevering on her chosen path.

Christ was for Clare the mirror in whose reflection she saw herself, others and the whole of reality. And there is one section of her Third Letter to Agnes of Prague that reveals the inward and outward, personal and global aspects and consequences of this reflected glory. 'You have taken hold of that incomparable treasure hidden in the field of the world and of the human heart'.[33] When the hidden treasure within the human heart is discovered, acknowledged and embraced, a whole new worldview opens. Infinite horizons replace narrow confines and limitations, because the heart's journey is expansive both inwards and outwards. We know that the deeper the roots of the tree, the wider its branches spread. This is very evident in Clare. She searched the depths of her own heart and through her daily gaze into the Christ mirror, she fully entered into the emerging levels from the periphery to the centre through poverty, humility and love. Sometimes we too have to start on the periphery, on the margins, before we can delve into or discover the centre. But once discovered, the centre, the true self, is the precious pearl of God's Indwelling in our own uniqueness, experienced in the human heart and in the field of the world.

Gazing into the heart of the God-man, Jesus Christ, Crucified and Glorious, suspended between heaven and earth and uniting them within himself, led Clare to enter ever more deeply into the mystery of communion and integration of all things human and divine. Clare understood and accepted the reality of identifying with her Crucified Spouse. In this sense she too experienced within her own life the trials and tribulations which are part and parcel of bearing the burden of broken humanity. She brought the familiar spousal imagery to greater depths, depths that participated in both the agony and the ecstasy of her Beloved, and she encouraged her sisters to do likewise.

If you suffer with Him, you will reign with Him.
If you weep with Him, you shall rejoice with Him;
If you die with Him on the Cross of tribulation,
You shall possess heavenly mansions in the splendour of
    the saints,
And in the Book of Life your name shall be called
    glorious among men.[34]

From the depths of her mystical experience, Clare was empowered to reach out to those around her, both in her community and in the wider world of need. Her warm and generous heart readily responded to suffering, distress and danger, by healing the wounds of those who sought in her the healing touch of Christ. Clare in her poverty met the lavishness of God, Who filled her with resources beyond her own strength. In her we find a new leader of women whose prophetic influence was steeped in her mystical experience.

Clare the New Leader of Women

The newness that Clare brought to the Church and the world was prophesied by Francis and proclaimed and confirmed by Pope Alexander IV. After his own dramatic conversion, Francis prophesied that an Order of holy virgins would be established at San Damiano who would make famous a way of life that would glorify the Father and restore his Kingdom on earth. On her deathbed, Clare remembered this prophecy and knew it had been fulfilled in her and in her sisters. With her usual simplicity and humility, Clare acknowledged that all is gift and she attributed the fulfilment of the prophecy to the kindness of God and his choice of her and her sisters. In the *Bull of Canonisation*, these words of Pope Alexander attest to the outstanding holiness and influence of Clare. 'Therefore let Mother Church rejoice because she had begotten and reared a daughter who, as a parent fruitful with virtues, has produced many daughters for Religious Life by her example'.[35]

Clare was the first woman in history to write a Rule of Life and have it approved by the Church. It took long years of prayer and perseverance to achieve this, but Clare never compromised her original and unique calling. She realised that her vocation was received anew each day.

> Among the other gifts that we have received and do daily receive from our Benefactor, the Father of Mercies, and for which we must express the deepest thanks to the glorious Father of Christ, there is our vocation, for which, all the more by way of its being more perfect and greater, we do owe the greatest thanks to Him.[36]

If we believe our vocation is received anew each day, then our hearts are open to the newness that this implies. Our vocation is not a 'once-and-for-all' moment. It is rather a daily invitation to live abundantly in the lavishness of God's infinite giving, which will always be beyond us, and always be new to those who have eyes to see. Only love makes such seeing possible.

The Primacy of Love

When I reflect on the vocation of Francis and Clare, my own vocation and the vocation of those I have accompanied on their faith journey, I am always led back to the primacy of love. 'What Francis and Clare will teach us is love; not only how to love God but how lovable God is, not only how to catch fire from God but how fiery God can be'.[37] The emphasis is always on love. It was the fire of love that transformed Francis when he received the stigmata. It was the fire of love that transformed Clare as she gazed, considered, contemplated and imitated her Crucified and Glorious Spouse. When that same love takes hold of us, we too, mystical and prophetic men and women like Francis and Clare, will penetrate the mystery of things with new eyes and a new heart. And in the power of that love we will be empowered to reach out to the margins, healing the wounds of our brothers and sisters and restoring Mother Earth. Like Francis and Clare, we too will realise the wonderful truth expressed by Franciscan friar, Joe Chinnici, where he says:

> The world is not poor; it is rich in God's goodness, image and likeness. Jesus restores it, recreates it, by becoming poor and relying on God's abundance in the world to feed and clothe Him. Jesus redeems, performs salvific activity, not by giving but by receiving, thus revealing to the world and to the people at the same time as He is redeeming it, the goodness of God.[38]

The ability to receive the goodness of God brings us back to the perennial Gospel truth which Jesus personified. 'In truth I tell you, unless you change and become like little children you will never enter the Kingdom of Heaven' (Mt 18:3). This is the secret of the Saints and Our Lady Queen of All Saints. They understood poverty and humility, and lovingly received from the abundance of God. Like Mary, we too can say 'My soul proclaims the greatness of the Lord and my spirit rejoices in God my Saviour; for the Almighty has done great things for me. Holy is his name' (Lk 1:46–49). Our Blessed Lady, the Saints, our Founders and Foundresses, all point to the way in which trust, openness, surrender and love leave God free to express himself within the human person in 'holy newness' that far surpass our human understanding or finite horizons. As Pope Francis said during the Beatification of Pope Paul VI, 'God is not afraid of new things! That is why he is continually surprising us, opening our hearts and guiding us in unexpected ways'.[39] The question remains: Where do we stand regarding God's surprising ways?

Pope Francis and Newness

Pope Francis in choosing Francis of Assisi as the Patron of his Pontificate seems to echo in our day, the papal joy of Pope Gregory IX when he canonised Francis. Celano tells us 'He rejoiced and exulted, dancing with joy, for in his own day he was seeing the Church of God being renewed with new mysteries that were ancient wonders'.[40] Pope Francis seems to have ushered in a 'holy newness' in the Church and the world through his personal witness and words of wisdom. Perhaps many of us experienced our hearts burning within us when Pope Francis challenged us to open our lives to the transforming power and newness of the Holy Spirit.

We fear that God may force us to strike out on new paths
and leave behind our all too narrow, closed and selfish
horizons in order to become open to his own. Yet
throughout the history of salvation, whenever God
reveals himself, he brings newness – God always brings
newness – and demands our complete trust.[41]

These timely words of Pope Francis challenge, invite
and inspire us in ways that are very demanding and
relevant to Religious Life. There is the invitation to leave
behind narrow horizons and to strike out on new paths.
There is the challenge to open our hearts and our lives
and to trust completely in the leading of God. This may
sound simplistic but when we look at what might be
involved for us as individuals or communities, there is a
radical stance that is as attractive as it is fearful.

Bearing in mind what we have already said in
previous chapters, if our lives are founded on the Rock,
which is Christ, we will continually discover the
meaning and depth of our personal and unique vocation
in him, which will determine our present and our future.
A growing intimacy with Christ and complete trust in
his Providence is the only way to live the mystery of our
continuing transformation, and through us, the transformation of our world. The foundation of this transformation is love. As St Paul says, everything else will
fail but love endures forever.

Religious Life and Newness

Our Founders and Foundresses were people of great
love, vision, courage and spiritual genius. When
speaking of the spiritual genius of St Francis, Richard

Rohr attributes it to Francis's eagerness to love.[42] But love opens us to continuous conversion and change and few people are comfortable with change. The familiar feels secure, but not to venture beyond our comfort zones leads to stagnation both personally and communally. As we have stressed numerous times throughout this chapter, God is always new. As Scripture says, 'Look, I am doing something new, now it emerges; can you not see it?' (Is 43:19).

Francis and Clare of Assisi, impelled by the power of the Spirit and the attraction of Jesus, totally surrendered to the infinite horizons that moved their hearts and changed their lives. Unafraid of leaving behind the tried and familiar in both Church and society, they bravely set out on a course that would change the world forever. Their followers recognised their 'newness' and left a written legacy to inspire us to believe that we too are called into the mystery of the Living God who is eternally doing a new thing. In every age, 'Religious Life is meant to embody in itself a Trinitarian ecclesial and social catechesis'.[43] This is the basis for a new evangelisation. 'The new evangelisation, like that of all times, will be effective if it proclaims from the rooftops what it has first lived in intimacy with the Lord'.[44]

Like our founders and foundresses, we too need to find ways of being in dialogue with the contemporary world in a way that 'both reaffirms the distinctiveness of the vowed Religious Life and prophetically witnesses to human social transformation'.[45] This was spelled out in *Vita Consecrata* as a major challenge facing Religious Life today.[46]

When I reflect on the gift of Religious Life in the

Church, I am drawn to the promise and reality that newness evokes and creates, while at the same time preserving the unchanging essence that is intrinsic to the gift. 'Every scribe who becomes a disciple of the Kingdom of Heaven is like a householder who brings out from his storeroom new things as well as old' (Mt 13:52). St Francis seems to embody this Gospel paradox, thus creating an original expression of radical discipleship. The Franciscan writer, Richard Rohr, sums it up by saying:

> Francis was traditional as well as entirely new in the ways of holiness, and he is still such a standing paradox. He stood barefoot on the earth and yet touched the heavens. He was grounded in the Church and yet instinctively moved towards the cosmos. He lived happily inside the visible and yet both suffered and rejoiced in what others thought was invisible. Again and again, he was totally at home in two worlds at the same time, and thus he made them one world.[47]

This he and Clare could do because the poor, chaste and obedient Christ was the Rock on which they built their lives, and amidst the changing sands of politics and religion, culture and economics, that marked their generation, Francis and Clare remained steadfast in simplicity and joy, following the poor and humble Christ. Popes and Bishops recognised their orthodoxy, and men, women and children were attracted by their newness. Celano described Francis as pouring out streams of the Gospel in a holy flood over the whole world, and he recognised in him a holy newness that brought new life and joy to the People of God. 'In him and though him, an unexpected joy and holy newness came into the world. A shoot of the ancient religion suddenly renewed the old and decrepit'.[48] A similar description sums up the influence of Clare. 'The ageing world was almost oppressed by the weight of years, the vision of faith faltering in the darkness, the footing of morals slipping away' when God in his kindness raised up 'a newness of sacred Orders' who would be 'lights of the world, leaders of the way and teachers of life'.[49] This threefold challenge is no less real today. 'The theological vision, community structures, and social mission are deeply interconnected'.[50] The mystics and prophets in our midst will recognise this interconnectedness and witness to it. This will always be the challenge facing Religious Life in every era, and its expression will always have a new face depending on the times in which we live.

In God, everything is new, and both Francis and Clare mirrored this newness in their own unique response to the God who awaited their personal love response and transformed them as they surrendered totally to that love. Pope Francis speaks of our openness to new paths and the promise and fulfilment that await such a response. 'The newness which God brings into our life is something that actually brings fulfilment, that gives true joy, true serenity, because God loves us and desires only our good'.[51] He also highlighted resistance to change and newness, especially regarding transient structures that have lost their capacity for openness to what is new. This is a real challenge to any community. The eternal and the transient often vie for equality and survival, and it takes the mystic and the prophet to recognise, face and embrace the tension and change that such awareness necessitates.

> Precisely because both Jesus and Francis were 'conserva-tives', in the true sense of the term, they conserved what was worth conserving – the core, the transformative life of the Gospel – and did not let accidentals get in the way, which are the very things false conservatives usually idolize. They then ended up looking quite 'progressive', radical, and even dangerous to the status quo.[52]

The Rock and the shifting sands will always be with us. How we live this mystery and paradox has tremendous and eternal consequences. Clare and Francis of Assisi incarnated newness in ways that revolutionised the Church and Religious Life in their day. This they did because they were first and foremost intimate with the Divine Spouse. 'Divine intimacy is more than enough to live on, and makes poverty, celibacy, and obedience no burden. But without such regular mirroring, these values cannot really be lived or loved, but only create bachelors and old maids'.[53]

Which are we?

Reflection

Do you experience Religious Life as a new and radical Gospel Way of sharing, loving and governing? Does it open you up to an alternative and transformative way of relating to every person as brother and sister in dialogue and solidarity?

Notes

1 Pope Benedict XVI, *Deus Caritas Est*, 1.
2 P. Jordan, *An Affair of the Heart, A Biblical and Franciscan Journey.* Leominster: Gracewing, 2008, p, 7.
3 P. Arrupe, SJ, *In Him Alone Our Hope.* Dublin: Irish Messenger Publications, 1981, p. 61.
4 Ibid., pp. 61–2.
5 R. Rohr, *On-Line Daily Meditations*, 1 October 2014.
6 Pope Benedict XVI, *Deus Caritas Est*, 1.
7 Ibid., 15.
8 Pope John Paul II, *Apostolic Exhortation Redemptionis Donum,* Vatican, 1984, 7.
9 R. Rohr, *Eager to Love, The Alternative Way of Francis of Assisi.* London: Hodder & Stoughton, 2014, p. xx.
10 W. J. Short, OFM, 'Francis, The "New" Saint in the Tradition of Christian Hagiography', in J. Hammond (editor), *Francis of Assisi, History, Hagiography and Hermeneutics in the Early Tradition.* London: New City, 2004, p. 153.
11 R. J. Armstrong, OFMCap., *et al, Francis of Assisi, The Saint, Early Documents*, vol, 1, p. 243.
12 Cf. W. J. Short, OFM, 'Francis, The "New" Saint in the Tradition of Christian Hagiography', pp. 153–4.
13 R. J. Armstrong, OFMCap., *et al*, vol. 1, p. 260.
14 Ibid., p. 202.
15 Ibid., p. 262.
16 Ibid., pp. 159–60.
17 Pope John Paul II, *Address in Lisieux*, 1980.
18 R. J. Armstrong, OFMCap., *et al*, vol, 1, p. 216.
19 Ibid., p. 220.
20 Ibid., p. 217.
21 Ibid., p. 255.
22 Ibid., p. 255.
23 W. J., Short, OFM, 'Francis, The "New" Saint in the Tradition of Christian Hagiography', in J. Hammond (editor), *Francis of Assisi, History, Hagiography and Hermeneutics in the Early Tradition.* London: New City, 2004, p. 162.
24 R. J. Armstrong, OFMCap., *et al*, vol. 1, p. 280.
25 Ibid., p. 282.
26 R. J. Armstrong, OFM Cap., *Clare of Assisi, Early Documents.* New

York: Paulist Press, 1988, p. 193.

27 Ibid., p. 197.
28 Ibid., p. 178.
29 *The Rule and Life of the Brothers and Sisters of the Third Order Regular of Saint Francis*, p. viii.
30 R. J. Armstrong, OFM Cap., *Clare of Assisi, Early Documents*, pp. 179–80.
31 Ibid., p. 44.
32 I. Delio, OSF, *Clare of Assisi, A Heart Full of Love*. Ohio: St Anthony Messenger Press, 2007, p. 31.
33 R. J. Armstrong, OFM Cap., *Clare of Assisi, Early Documents*, p. 44.
34 Ibid., p. 42.
35 Ibid., p. 182.
36 Ibid., p. 54.
37 Frances Teresa, OSC, *This Living Mirror, Reflections on Clare of Assisi*. London: Darton, Longman & Todd, 1995, p. 3.
38 J. P. Chinnici, OFM, 'Evangelical and Apostolic Tensions' in *Our Franciscan Charism Today*. USA: St Bonaventure University, 1987, p. 110.
39 Pope Francis, *Homily on the Beatification of Pope Paul VI*, Rome, 19 October 2014.
40 R. J. Armstrong, OFMCap., *et al*, vol, 1, p. 291.
41 Pope Francis, *Pentecost Homily*, 2013.
42 R. Rohr, *Eager to Love, The Alternative Way of Francis of Assisi*. London: Hodder & Stoughton, 2014.
43 M. Cusato, OFM & J. F.,Godet-Calogeras, (eds), *Vita Evangelica, Essays in Honour of Margaret Carney, OSF*. USA: The Franciscan Institute, 2006, p. 514.
44 Pope John Paul II, *Vita Consecrata*, 81.
45 M. Cusato, OFM & J. F. Godet-Calogeras, (eds), *Vita Evangelica, Essays in Honour of Margaret Carney, OSF*, p. 515.
46 Pope John Paul II, *Vita Consecrata*, 72–103.
47 R. Rohr, *Eager to Love, The Alternative Way of Francis of Assisi*, p. xvii.
48 R. J. Armstrong, OFMCap., *et al*, vol, 1, pp. 259–60.
49 R. J. Armstrong, OFM Cap., *Clare of Assisi, Early Documents*, pp. 187–8.
50 M. Cusato, OFM & J. F. Godet-Calogeras, (eds.), *Vita Evangelica, Essays in Honour of Margaret Carney, OSF*, p. 514.
51 Pope Francis, *Pentecost Homily*, 2013.

52 R. Rohr, *Eager to Love, The Alternative Way of Francis of Assisi*, p. xx.
53 Ibid., p. 142.

Conclusion

*In calling you God says to you: 'You are important to me,
I love you, I am counting on you'.*[1]

This book has been a labour of love. Started in the Year
of Faith 2012, I had hoped to complete it that same year.
However, Congregational commitments made that
impossible. During the intervening time, I was delighted
when Pope Francis announced the Year of Consecrated
Life, which makes my personal and limited reflection
timely. As previously mentioned, I wanted to present
Religious Life with a sense of Jubilee celebration,
acknowledging the precious gift of Consecrated Life in
the Church.

In *Rejoice*, a Letter to consecrated men and women in
preparation for the Year of Consecrated Life, Pope
Francis invites us on an 'interior pilgrimage, ... to make
our whole life a pilgrimage of loving transformation'.[2]
He emphasises that this interior pilgrimage begins with
prayer, the source of our fruitfulness in mission. The
indescribable mystery of our call and vocation, Pope
Francis says, can only be interpreted in faith. When faith
is lacking, then life loses meaning and faces of our
brothers and sisters are obscured. This insistence on
faith echoes the words of Pope Benedict with which I

began this reflection where he urged us to make an inner pilgrimage to rediscover our first love, that moment of recognising the call to radical love when Jesus set our hearts on fire. As Sister Wendy Beckett says in one of her Letters: 'First fervour and honeymoon happiness are beginnings – they never, never pass, if we let them work on us. They will grow and deepen. Our happiness is because we now belong to God'.[3]

Tracing this journey through my own limited experience and perception, I now arrive at a moment when, with even greater joy and gratitude, I desire anew 'to take up Jesus's way of life, to adopt his interior attitude, to allow myself to be invaded by his Spirit, to absorb his surprising logic and his scale of values, to share in his risks and hopes'.[4] And in this Year of Consecrated Life such an opportunity is offered to every Religious. Pope Francis has called us to 'wake up the world' by living differently and with true joy that is contagious and infections. It propels us forward to meet the needs of our brothers and sisters in closeness and encounter, in the newness of the Gospel.[5]

Throughout this reflection, I have emphasised the mystical and prophetic dimensions of Religious Life. 'Contemplation expands into prophetic aptitude. The prophet is one whose eye is opened, and who hears and speaks the words of God; a person of three times: the promise of the past, the contemplation of the present, the courage to point out the path toward the future'.[6] In this sense, we have rejoiced in our God-given charisms, gifted to our Founders and Foundresses in the past, which we now share and interpret for our times. Contemplating the present, we read the signs of the times and allow our different charisms to creatively shape and transform our world, in us and through us. This in turn will point us toward the future, in which we will strive to be a therapy for humanity, and a blessing for our world.

As I come to the end of this short book, I feel a deep resonance with the words of Mary in her Magnificat, glorifying the Lord, who continues to work wonders as we welcome with great joy and openness, the gift of the Year of Consecrated Life. With eagerness and enthusiasm let us humbly receive God's graces, gifts, challenges and changes that this Year opens to us, praying: 'Glory be to him whose power, working in us, can do infinitely more than we can ask or imagine; glory be to him from generation to generation in the Church and in Christ Jesus for ever and ever. Amen' (Eph 3:20–1).

Notes

1 Pope Francis, *Rejoice! A Message from the Teachings of Pope Francis. A Letter to Consecrated Men and Women in Preparation for the Year Dedicated to Consecrated Life,* London: CTS Publication, 2014, p. 16.

2 Ibid., p. 17.

3 W. Beckett, Sister, *Spiritual Letters,* London: Bloomsbury, 2013, p. 233.

4 Pope Francis, *Rejoice! A Message from the Teachings of Pope Francis. A Letter to Consecrated Men and Women in Preparation for the Year Dedicated to Consecrated Life,* London: CTS Publication, 2014, p. 20.

5 Ibid., pp. 35–6.

6 Ibid., p. 25.

Articles

Aschenbrenner, SJ, G., 'Active and Monastic: Two Apostolic Lifestyles', in *Review for Religious*, Sept/Oct 1986, pp. 653–88.

Benedict XVI, Pope, *Homily for the Presentation of Our Lord*. Rome, 2013.

Blastic, OFMConv., M., 'It Pleases Me That You Should Teach Sacred Theology, Franciscans Doing Theology', in *Franciscan Studies*, 55, 1998, pp. 1–25.

Bodo, OFM, M., St Francis the Practical Mystic, http://www.americancatholic.org/features/special Date of Access, 22/10/14.

Chinnici, J., 'Evangelical and Apostolic Tensions,' in *Our Franciscan Charism Today*. New Jersey: Fame, 1987.

Chinnici, J., 'The Prophetic Heart: The Evangelical Form of Religious Life in the United States', Keynote Address 29th Annual Franciscan Federation Conference, Chicago, 1994.

Corriveau, OFMCap., J., 'Evangelical Brotherhood' in *Circular Letter 11*. Rome, 1997.

Delio, I., 'Evangelical Life Today: Living in the Ecological Christ', in *Franciscan Studies*, 64, 2006, pp. 475–506.

Francis, Pope, *Address to the Union of Superiors General*. Rome, 2013.

Francis, Pope, *Homily on the Beatification of Pope Paul VI*. Rome, 2014.

Francis, Pope, *Message for the Year of Consecrated Life*. Rome, 2014.

Francis, Pope, *New Year's Day Angelus Address*. Rome, 2014.

Francis, Pope, *Pentecost Homily*, Rome, 2013.

Franciscan Federation of the Third Order Regular, *Response to the Lineamenta in the Light of the 1994 Synod of Bishops on Consecrated Life*, 1994.

Garcia, ODC, C., 'Mysticism and Prophecy, A Style of Life and New Areopagus', *Plenary Assembly of UISG*. Rome, 2010.

Godet, J. F., 'Clare the Woman, as Seen in her Writings', in *Greyfriars Review*, 4/3. USA: St Bonaventure University, 1990, pp. 7–30.

Higgins, OFM, M., 'Active-Contemplative Synthesis', in *The Cord*, 46/5, 1995.

Ingham, M. B., 'The Logic of the Gift: Clare of Assisi and Franciscan Evangelical Life', in *The Cord*, 60/3, 2010, pp. 243–56.

Jamison, OSB, C., 'The Future Depends on the Possibility of Dialogue between the Old and the New Orders', in *The Tablet*, April, 2002.

John Paul II, Pope, *Address in Lisieux*, 1980.

John Paul II, Pope, *Address to the Conference Studying the Implementation of the Second Vatican Council*. Rome, 2000.

Moffatt, OSF, K., *Franciscan Evangelical Life*, Presentation at FSM General Chapter, 2009.

Radcliffe, OP, T., *The Identity of Religious Today*, Keynote Address US Conference of Major Superiors for Men, 1996.

Rohr, OFM, R., *On-Line Daily Meditations*, 1 October 2014.

Schlosser, M., 'Mother, Sister, Bride: The Spirituality of Saint Clare', in *Greyfriars Review*, vol, 5/2. USA: St Bonaventure University, 1991, pp. 233–49.

Secondin, O Carm, B., 'The Almond Branch and the Boiling Pot', *UISG Address*. Rome, 2010.

Short, OFM, W., 'Give an Account of the Hope that Lies Within You', in *The Cord*, 53/5, 203, pp. 252–9.

Bibliography

Armstrong, OFMCap., R. J., (edited and translated), *Clare of Assisi: Early Documents*. NY: Paulist Press, 1988.

Armstrong, OFMCap., R. J., & Brady, OFM, I. C., (trans.), *Francis and Clare, The Complete Works*. NY: Paulist Press, 1982.

Armstrong, OFMCap., R. J., Hellmann, OFMConv., W. J. A., Short, OFM., W. J., *Francis of Assisi, The Saint, Early Documents*, vol. 1. London, New York: New City Press, 1999.

Armstrong, OFMCap., R. J., Hellmann, OFMConv., W. J. A., Short, OFM, W. J., *Francis of Assisi, The Founder, Early Documents*, vol. 2. London, New York: New City Press, 2000.

Armstrong, OFMCap., R. J., Hellmann, OFMConv., W. J. A., Short, OFM, W. J., *Francis of Assisi, The Prophet, Early Documents*, vol. 3. London, New York: New City Press, 2001.

Arrupe, SJ, P., *In Him Alone Our Hope*. Dublin: Irish Messenger Press, 1981.

Benedict XVI, Pope, *Deus Caritas Est*. Vatican, 2005.

Benedict XVI, Pope, *Porta Fidei*. Vatican, 2011.

Bodo, OFM, M., *Mystics: 10 Who Show Us the Way to God*. Cincinnati: St Anthony Messenger Press, 2007.

Burrows, OCD, R., *Essence of Prayer*. London: Burns & Oates, 2006.

Chittester, OSB, J., *The Fire in These Ashes, A Spirituality of Contemporary Religious Life*. Leominister: Gracewing, 1995.

Chittester, OSB, J., *Religious life is still alive, but far from the*

Promised Land: Ten Questions get to Heart of what the Future Might Hold. USA: Catholic Reporter, 1994.

Code of Canon Law. London: Collins Liturgical Publications, 1983.

Congregation for Institutes of Consecrated Life and Societies of Apostolic Life, *Rejoice! A Message from the Teachings of Pope Francis. A Letter to Consecrated Men and Women in Preparation for the Year Dedicated to Consecrated Life.* London: CTS, 2014.

Congregation for Institutes of Consecrated Life and Societies of Apostolic Life, Instruction, *Starting Afresh from Christ: A Renewed Commitment to Consecrated Life in the Third Millennium.* London: CTS, 2002.

Cusato, OFM, M. F., & Godet-Calogeras, J. F., (editors), *Vita Evangelica*, Essays in Honour of Margaret Carney, OSF. USA: The Franciscan Institute, 2006.

Flannery, OP, A., *Vatican Council II The Conciliar and Post Conciliar Documents.* Leominster: Fowler Wright Books Ltd, 1981.

Flannery, OP, A., *Vatican Council II More Post Conciliar Documents,* vol, 2. Leominster: Fowler Wright Books Ltd, 1982.

Frances Teresa, OSC, *This Living Mirror, Reflections on Clare of Assisi.* London: Darton, Longman & Todd, 1995.

Francis, Pope, *Keep Watch! A Letter to Consecrated Men and Women Journeying in the Footsteps of God.* Congregation for Institutes of Consecrated Life and Societies of Apostolic Life. London: CTS, 2014.

Grun, A., *Jesus The Image of Humanity, Luke's Account.* London: Continuum, 2003.

Hammond, J., (ed.), *Francis of Assisi, History, Hagiography and Hermeneutics in the Early Documents.* London: New City Press, 2004.

Harris, M., *Proclaim Jubilee, A Spirituality for the Twenty-First Century.* Kentucky: Westminster John Knox Press, 1996.

Jamison, OSB, C., (ed.), *The Disciples' Call: Theologies of Vocation from Scripture to the Present Day.* London: Bloomsbury, 2013.

John Paul II, Pope, *Redemptoris Hominis*. Vatican, 1979.

John Paul II, Pope, *Redemptionis Donum*. Vatican, 1984.

John Paul II, Pope, *Vita Consecrata, The Consecrated Life and its Mission in the Church and in the World*. London: CTS, 1996

Jordan, FSM, P., *An Affair of the Heart, A Biblical and Franciscan Journey*. Leominster: Gracewing, 2008.

Lapsanski, D., *Evangelical Perfection, An Historical Examination of the Concept in the Early Sources*. USA: The Franciscan Institute, 1977.

Pacomio, L., *Jubilee in the Bible*. Vatican Publications, 2000.

Pontifical Work for Ecclesiastical Vocations, *New Vocations for a New Europe*. Vatican, 1997.

Ratzinger, Cardinal, J., *God and the World*. San Francisco: Ignatius Press, 2000.

Rivi, OFMCap., P., *This is Me, A Journey Through the Sources to Discover the Real Francis*. Italy: Edizioni Porziuncula, 2011.

Rode, F., Archbishop, *Reflection on the Occasion of the 40th Anniversary of Perfectae Caritatis*. Rome, 2005.

Rohr, OFM, R., *Eager to Love, The Alternative Way of Francis of Assisi*. London: Hodder & Stoughton, 2014.

Rule and Life of the Brothers and Sisters of the Third Order Regular of Saint Francis. Rome, 1982.

Sacred Congregation for Religious and Secular Institutes, *Essential Elements in the Church's Teaching on Religious Life*. Vatican, 1983.

Sparado, SJ, J., 'Wake Up the World. Conversation with Pope Francis about Religious Life', in *La Civiltà Cattolica*, 2014.

Weigel, G., *Evangelical Catholicism, Deep Reform in the Twenty-First Century Church*. NY: Basic Books, 2013.

Lightning Source UK Ltd.
Milton Keynes UK
UKOW04f0327210115

244820UK00001B/68/P